With the hurricane gone, calm returns and places unlucky enough to be in its path slowly recover. But as long as the Sun keeps shining and pumping its warmth into the ocean, you can be sure that somewhere in the world, another storm is brewing...

A hurricane can be awesome in its power, but never lasts for more than a few weeks, at most. Eventually, its power will dwindle as it moves into cooler places, or crosses onto land where it is robbed of its supply of energy-giving moisture.

The hurricane's counterclockwise spin tells us that it is in the northern hemisphere, in the Atlantic, and is roaring westward to unleash its fury upon the coasts of the Caribbean and the Gulf of Mexico. Whole populations are now fleeing the region before the hurricane strikes.

A satellite detects a thick mass of spiral-shaped clouds—a hurricane moving across the ocean. This storm is vast—twice the size of the United Kingdom. The sheer power contained in its whirling winds is one of the mightiest forces in nature.

DK experience **EXTREME**

WEATHER

written by
JOHN FARNDON

THE SOLAR WEATHER MACHINE

All the world's weather begins far away in the glowing ball of the Sun. The Sun is a star, and, like all stars, it is incredibly hot. Deep in its fiery heart, the Sun's huge mass forces atoms together to generate unimaginable heat, as if in an ever-exploding nuclear bomb. Temperatures inside reach 27,000,000°F (15,000,000°C). Slowly but relentlessly, over 10 million years or so, all this heat burns its way out toward the Sun's surface, making it a raging inferno. This is the energy that drives the Earth's weather.

The Sun's surface, or **photosphere**, glows with amazing brightness. An area no bigger than a postage stamp is brighter than 1.5 million candles. The photosphere burns so brilliantly that it floodlights the entire **solar system**, beaming out heat and light nonstop in all directions at 186,000 miles (300,000 km) per second.

As the Sun's upper atmosphere, or **corona**, heats up, it pumps out electrically charged **particles**—more than a million tons of them every second. The particles stream out from the Sun in all directions at more than 250 miles (400 km) per second in what is called the solar wind.

In three minutes, the Sun's rays reach Mercury, scorching the planet's surface to more than 662°F (350°C). The solar wind has blown away any **atmosphere** on Mercury that might trap heat. So as soon as the planet's sunny side turns away from the Sun and into shadow, temperatures drop to a chilly -274°F (-170°C).

In 1975, Russia's *Venera* space probe spotted lightninglike flashes on Venus. Could Venus have thunderstorms like those on Earth, stirred up by the Sun heating the atmosphere? But no flashes have been seen since. Lightning may therefore be rare on Venus, caused only by volcanic eruptions.

Sunlight streams past Mercury and strikes Venus three minutes later. Here, sunlight boiled away any water long ago. With no water to soak it up, Venus' atmosphere is thick with **carbon dioxide** gas that belches from its volcanoes. Sunlight can get in, but its heat is trapped beneath thick clouds, heating the surface to 900°F (482°C).

photosphere The glowing surface of the Sun that radiates light throughout the solar system.

solar system The planets, including the Earth, and other objects that continually orbit around the Sun.

corona The Sun's incredibly hot, glowing atmosphere of gases.

particles The extremely tiny pieces, such as electrons, from which all matter is made.

Mars may not have weather like the Earth's, but it has dust storms so gigantic they can cover the entire planet. The surface of Mars is as dry and dusty as any desert on the Earth. Scientists think Mars's monster dust storms may begin when sunlight heats up the air, and also the dust in the air. This generates powerful air currents that pick up more dust, warming the air even more.

By the time it reaches Jupiter, sunlight is very weak. Jupiter, however, is so big that it has its own internal source of heat generated by immense pressures. This heat is enough to stir up winds of up to 400 mph (650 kph) and to set off lightning flashes 1,000 times as powerful as any on the Earth.

The Sun's rays are becoming weaker by the time they reach Mars. Nowhere on Mars gets remotely as warm as the warmest places on the Earth. The cold places are much colder, plummeting to -207°F (-133°C). There is too little moisture for clouds to develop, so Mars has almost no weather.

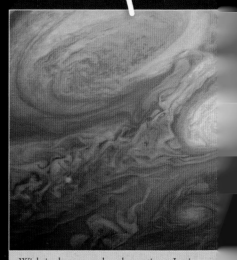

With its honey and amber stripes, Jupiter is a beautiful planet. Its distinctive Great Red Spot is a swirl in Jupiter's atmosphere, which scientists believe is a hurricane that has lasted for more than 300 years. But this hurricane is so large—more than 25,000 miles (40,000 km) across—that it could engulf all of the Earth.

After just eight minutes, sunlight hits the Earth, passing down into its atmosphere and filling it with the heat energy that drives our weather. Meanwhile, the charged particles of the solar wind are hurtling earthward, too. Four days after leaving the Sun, they rush past the Earth.

As the Sun's energy spreads throughout the solar system, its heat stirs clouds of gas into motion on any planet that has an atmosphere. It is this motion of the atmosphere that gives us everything we call weather.

atmosphere The blanket of gases covering the surface of a planet.

carbon dioxide A gas created by burning, by living things, and by volcanoes.

Sparks fly as solar particles cannon into the particles of the atmosphere. Brilliant flashes of light flare out in the sky around the polar cleft, creating a spectacular display of shimmering colors. Called the **aurora** australis, or southern lights, this beautiful phenomenon is visible in the southern sky surrounding the South Pole.

Like water down a drain, the solar wind's charged particles hurtle down the walls of the cleft toward the South Pole. At first, they meet no opposition. Then, about 150 miles (250 km) up, they crash into the first particles of gas that make up Earth's atmosphere.

Occasionally, however, an outburst on the Sun creates a gust in the solar wind, called a solar storm. The magnetosphere protects Earth from the worst, but it has two weak points—funnel-shaped clefts over the North and South poles. As the storm roars past, some charged particles spiral in through these clefts toward the planet's surface.

Radioactive particles in the solar wind could be deadly to life on Earth. Fortunately, our planet is protected by the magnetosphere (see box opposite). Deflected by the magnetosphere, most of the torrent of dangerous particles washes around Earth harmlessly, like a stream around a rock.

aurora The light created by air colliding with the charged particles of the solar wind as they enter the atmosphere over the poles.

From the ground, we see an intense glow beyond the horizon. For a few minutes, it arches up into the sky. Then new arcs of light curve up below it. Suddenly, an **auroral substorm** surges in. At once, bands of colored light appear, wavering high in the air like a curtain blown in the wind.

The southern lights hover in a great oval-shaped ring all around the South Pole, called the **auroral oval**. It lies roughly along the line of the polar circle, and from space looks like the flame of a gigantic gas ring. The whole display lasts 20 minutes or so, before fading out as the surge of particles from the solar wind dies down.

When particles in the solar wind strike the various gases in the atmosphere, they make each glow a different color. When solar particles crash into nitrogen, for example, the nitrogen sparks out in brilliant bursts of crimson or blue. Where nitrogen is mixed in different states, rippling purple fringes may appear.

Sometimes solar particles reach oxygen in the atmosphere, causing it to glow a brilliant yellow-green. Higher up, the oxygen flares into the rarer, vivid red aurorae.

MAGNETOSPHERE

The Earth is in fact an enormous, low-powered magnet. The magnetosphere is an extension of the Earth's magnetic field, which stretches 40,000 miles (65,000 km) out into space. The magnetosphere shelters the Earth from the blast of the solar wind, which distorts the magnetosphere into the shape of a comet. On the "downwind" side of the Earth, the magnetosphere stretches out in a gigantic tail 250,000 miles (400,000 km) long.

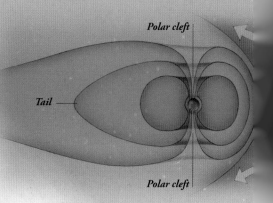

Polar cleft

Tail

Polar cleft

auroral substorm A hailstorm of electrically charged particles generating varieties of intense color.

auroral oval The ring formed by the aurorae over the Earth's magnetic poles.

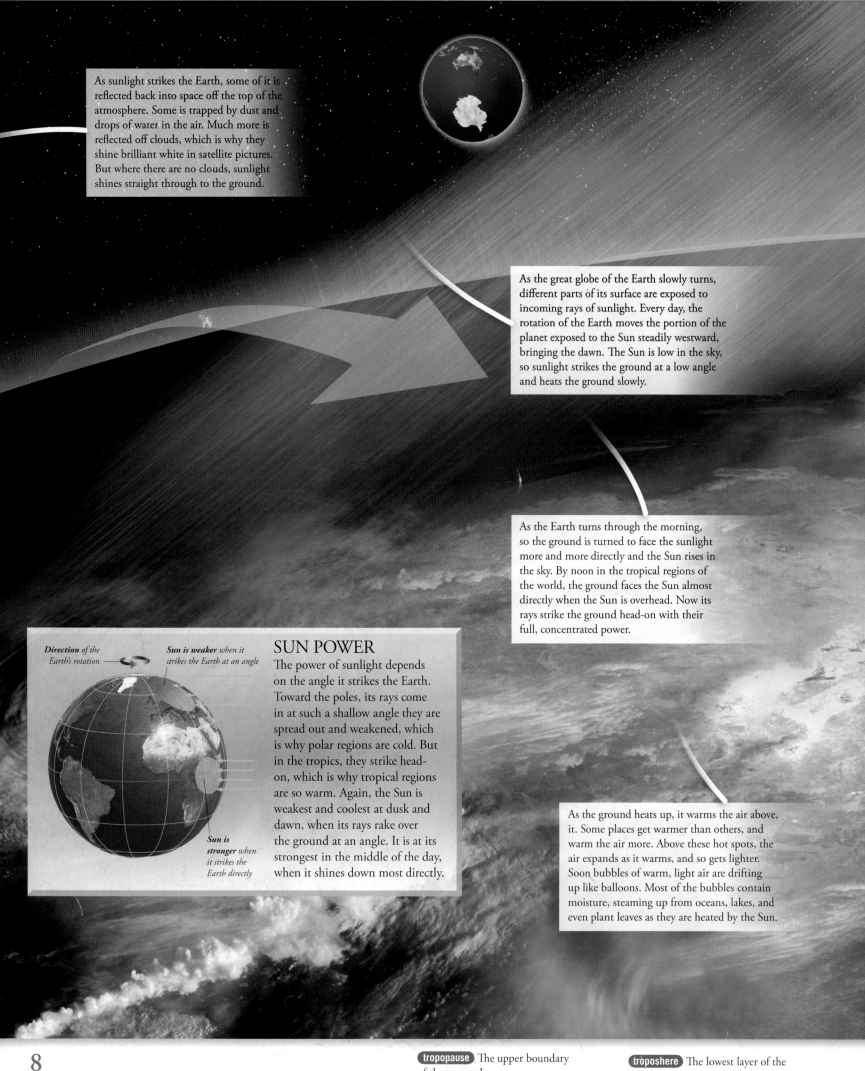

As sunlight strikes the Earth, some of it is reflected back into space off the top of the atmosphere. Some is trapped by dust and drops of water in the air. Much more is reflected off clouds, which is why they shine brilliant white in satellite pictures. But where there are no clouds, sunlight shines straight through to the ground.

As the great globe of the Earth slowly turns, different parts of its surface are exposed to incoming rays of sunlight. Every day, the rotation of the Earth moves the portion of the planet exposed to the Sun steadily westward, bringing the dawn. The Sun is low in the sky, so sunlight strikes the ground at a low angle and heats the ground slowly.

As the Earth turns through the morning, so the ground is turned to face the sunlight more and more directly and the Sun rises in the sky. By noon in the tropical regions of the world, the ground faces the Sun almost directly when the Sun is overhead. Now its rays strike the ground head-on with their full, concentrated power.

SUN POWER

Direction of the Earth's rotation

Sun is weaker when it strikes the Earth at an angle

Sun is stronger when it strikes the Earth directly

The power of sunlight depends on the angle it strikes the Earth. Toward the poles, its rays come in at such a shallow angle they are spread out and weakened, which is why polar regions are cold. But in the tropics, they strike head-on, which is why tropical regions are so warm. Again, the Sun is weakest and coolest at dusk and dawn, when its rays rake over the ground at an angle. It is at its strongest in the middle of the day, when it shines down most directly.

As the ground heats up, it warms the air above, it. Some places get warmer than others, and warm the air more. Above these hot spots, the air expands as it warms, and so gets lighter. Soon bubbles of warm, light air are drifting up like balloons. Most of the bubbles contain moisture, steaming up from oceans, lakes, and even plant leaves as they are heated by the Sun.

tropopause The upper boundary of the troposphere.

troposhere The lowest layer of the atmosphere—the only one containing the moisture that gives clouds and weather.

Exosphere
430–500 miles
(691–800 km)

Thermosphere
54–430 miles
(87–690 km)

Mesosphere
31–54 miles
(50–87 km)

Stratosphere
11–31 miles
(18–50 km)

Troposphere
0–11 miles
(0–18 km)

LAYERS OF THE ATMOSPHERE

The atmosphere has five layers. The lowest, the troposphere, contains 75 percent of the atmosphere's gases, and is cooler toward the top. Higher up is the stratosphere. Here temperatures rise with height because the layer contains ozone gas, which absorbs ultraviolet sunlight. Higher still is the mesosphere. Here the air is too thin to intercept the Sun's rays, and temperatures drop with height again. Beyond this is the thermosphere, which is so exposed to the Sun that temperatures soar to 3,600°F (2,000°C). Finally, nearly 430 miles (700 km) up, is the exosphere, where gases are so thin they drift off into space.

Up to a level called the tropopause, the air gets cooler as it gets higher, but then it starts to get hotter. Warm air can never carry moisture up beyond this ceiling. So all the atmosphere's moisture is trapped below, in the lowest layer of the atmosphere, called the troposphere. It is in this layer that all the world's weather happens.

As more and more bubbles of warm air drift upward, the masses and masses of water droplets begin to gather into white clouds. This happens wherever the energy of sunlight on the ground heats any moist air above. As a result, clouds appear all over the world, constantly changing and shifting as the effect of the Sun varies.

The atmosphere gets thinner higher up. So as the bubbles of warm air drift up, they have room to swell even farther. As the air expands, its heat spreads out, cooling it. Every 330 ft (100 m) it rises, it gets 1.8°F (1°C) cooler, until any moisture the air contains condenses to form water droplets.

stratosphere The clear layer of the atmosphere above the tropopause. It contains the ozone layer.

mesosphere The layer of thin gases above the stratosphere in which aurorae appear.

thermosphere The hot layer of very thin gases above the mesosphere.

exosphere The outermost layer of the atmosphere.

CATALOG OF WEATHER-WATCHING INSTRUMENTS

Advances in space and computer technology mean that forecasters can now predict weather accurately days in advance. With satellites, they can monitor storms as they develop from small disturbances to monster hurricanes. Forecasters also rely on a constant stream of information about atmospheric conditions around the world. Day and night, a huge network of weather observatories is at work taking millions of measurements every three hours.

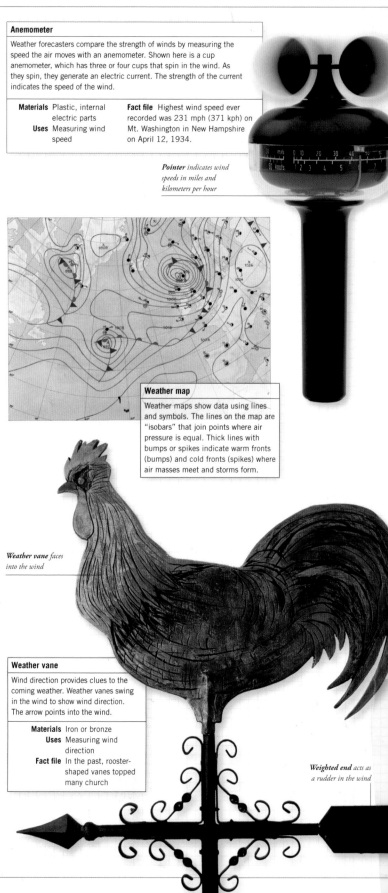

Anemometer

Weather forecasters compare the strength of winds by measuring the speed the air moves with an anemometer. Shown here is a cup anemometer, which has three or four cups that spin in the wind. As they spin, they generate an electric current. The strength of the current indicates the speed of the wind.

Materials	Plastic, internal electric parts	**Fact file** Highest wind speed ever recorded was 231 mph (371 kph) on Mt. Washington in New Hampshire on April 12, 1934.
Uses	Measuring wind speed	

Pointer indicates wind speeds in miles and kilometers per hour

Weather map

Weather maps show data using lines and symbols. The lines on the map are "isobars" that join points where air pressure is equal. Thick lines with bumps or spikes indicate warm fronts (bumps) and cold fronts (spikes) where air masses meet and storms form.

Weather vane faces into the wind

Weather vane

Wind direction provides clues to the coming weather. Weather vanes swing in the wind to show wind direction. The arrow points into the wind.

Materials	Iron or bronze	
Uses	Measuring wind direction	
Fact file	In the past, rooster-shaped vanes topped many church	

Weighted end acts as a rudder in the wind

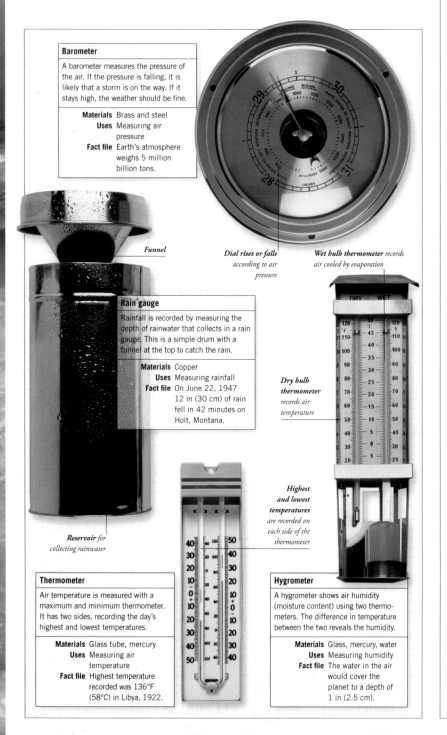

Barometer

A barometer measures the pressure of the air. If the pressure is falling, it is likely that a storm is on the way. If it stays high, the weather should be fine.

Materials	Brass and steel
Uses	Measuring air pressure
Fact file	Earth's atmosphere weighs 5 million billion tons.

Funnel

Dial rises or falls according to air pressure

Wet bulb thermometer records air cooled by evaporation

Rain gauge

Rainfall is recorded by measuring the depth of rainwater that collects in a rain gauge. This is a simple drum with a funnel at the top to catch the rain.

Materials	Copper
Uses	Measuring rainfall
Fact file	On June 22, 1947 12 in (30 cm) of rain fell in 42 minutes on Holt, Montana.

Dry bulb thermometer records air temperature

Reservoir for collecting rainwater

Highest and lowest temperatures are recorded on each side of the thermometer

Thermometer

Air temperature is measured with a maximum and minimum thermometer. It has two sides, recording the day's highest and lowest temperatures.

Materials	Glass tube, mercury
Uses	Measuring air temperature
Fact file	Highest temperature recorded was 136°F (58°C) in Libya, 1922.

Hygrometer

A hygrometer shows air humidity (moisture content) using two thermometers. The difference in temperature between the two reveals the humidity.

Materials	Glass, mercury, water
Uses	Measuring humidity
Fact file	The water in the air would cover the planet to a depth of 1 in (2.5 cm).

Stevenson screen

Air temperature and humidity readings must be taken in the shade. So thermometers are put inside white boxes to protect them from direct sunlight. Slats allow air to flow freely through the box, which also shelters other instruments from wind and rain.

Weather satellite

Satellites in space give an overview of the weather. "Radiometer" pictures show clouds around the world. Infrared pictures show temperatures and cloud patterns. Computers work out wind speeds from the way clouds move or light reflects off ocean waves. Geostationary satellites always sit in the same place above the Earth; polar orbiting satellites loop around the poles.

Uses Monitoring weather patterns and forecasting	**Fact file** The world's first weather satellite, Tiros I, was launched on April 1, 1960.

Transmitter sends data collected back to Earth

Reflective metallic foil protects instruments from radiation

Weather watching from the air

A useful way to get a close-up view of air conditions at different heights is in an aircraft. Special research aircraft equipped with an array of sensors often fly over storms to monitor them at close range. Some planes are designed to fly right into the eye of a hurricane.

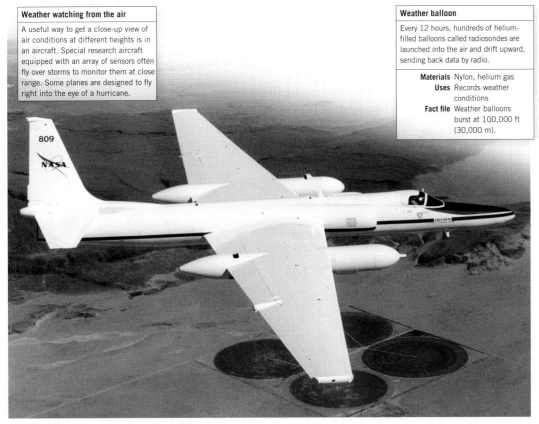

Weather balloon

Every 12 hours, hundreds of helium-filled balloons called radiosondes are launched into the air and drift upward, sending back data by radio.

Materials	Nylon, helium gas
Uses	Records weather conditions
Fact file	Weather balloons burst at 100,000 ft (30,000 m).

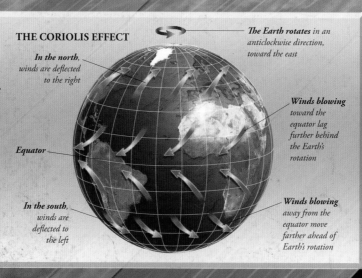

TROPICAL WINDS

Winds develop wherever the heat of the Sun stirs air into motion to create a difference in (air pressure)—blowing out from areas of high pressure where air is cool and sinking and into areas of low pressure where it is warm and rising. Near the equator, the Sun's heat is at its most powerful. Here its heat generates a gigantic wind machine that draws in winds from north and south, controlling the weather throughout the tropics.

Far to the north and to the south of the equator, these high-level winds roar through the upper air, unnoticed on the ground. Such is the power of the tropical sun that the winds blow several thousand miles into the subtropics. The air in these winds is cold, however, and eventually it begins to sink.

Meanwhile, as the rising air moves upward, it pushes air out of the way before it. This driven air cannot go any higher. Instead, it moves sideways, away from the equator—some to the north and some to the south. Soon winds are blowing high above the ground on either side of the equator.

Every morning as the tropical sun comes up, blazing heat is pumped into the Earth's surface. Over oceans and forests—wherever there is moisture— warm, moist air surges up throughout the morning. Soon huge clouds are piling up, often creating cloud bands stretching thousands of miles.

By midafternoon, the clouds tower some 7–9 miles (12–15 km) into the air. They become so thick with water that the air can no longer support their weight. Suddenly, with little warning, the clouds break and unleash a torrential shower of rain. The downpour is intense but rarely lasts longer than an hour or so.

MOVING AIR

Winds never flow directly from high to low pressure zones. Instead, they always (veer) to the right in the northern half of the world, and always to the left in the south, since they are affected by the spinning of the Earth. This is partly because the surface of the Earth is moving at its fastest at the equator, but is completely still at the poles. So air in winds starting at the poles lags more and more behind the Earth as it moves nearer the equator. With air moving away from the equator, however, it is the Earth that lags behind. This is known as the Coriolis effect.

THE CORIOLIS EFFECT

The Earth rotates in an anticlockwise direction, toward the east

In the north, winds are deflected to the right

Winds blowing toward the equator lag further behind the Earth's rotation

Equator

In the south, winds are deflected to the left

Winds blowing away from the equator move farther ahead of Earth's rotation

(air pressure) The pressure exerted by air in the atmosphere because of the weight of air above it.

(veer) Wind changing to a clockwise direction. (A wind changing to a counterclockwise direction is said to back.)

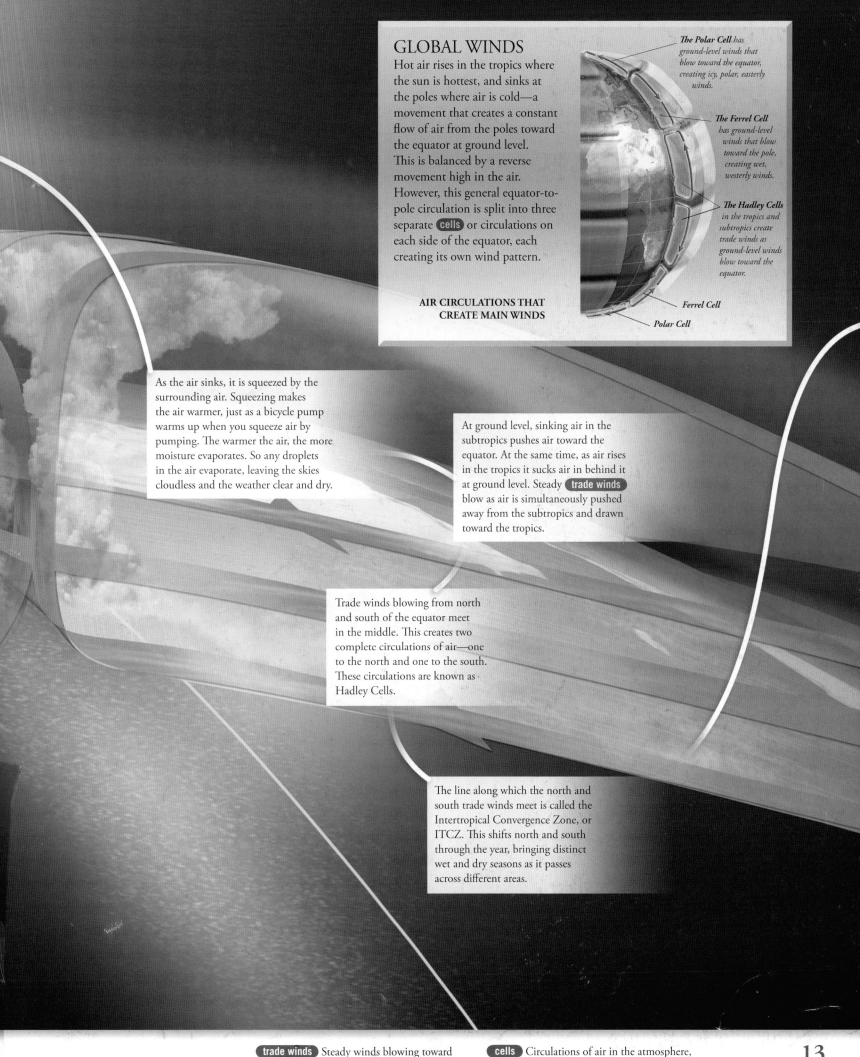

GLOBAL WINDS

Hot air rises in the tropics where the sun is hottest, and sinks at the poles where air is cold—a movement that creates a constant flow of air from the poles toward the equator at ground level. This is balanced by a reverse movement high in the air. However, this general equator-to-pole circulation is split into three separate cells or circulations on each side of the equator, each creating its own wind pattern.

The Polar Cell has ground-level winds that blow toward the equator, creating icy, polar, easterly winds.

The Ferrel Cell has ground-level winds that blow toward the pole, creating wet, westerly winds.

The Hadley Cells in the tropics and subtropics create trade winds as ground-level winds blow toward the equator.

Ferrel Cell

Polar Cell

AIR CIRCULATIONS THAT CREATE MAIN WINDS

As the air sinks, it is squeezed by the surrounding air. Squeezing makes the air warmer, just as a bicycle pump warms up when you squeeze air by pumping. The warmer the air, the more moisture evaporates. So any droplets in the air evaporate, leaving the skies cloudless and the weather clear and dry.

At ground level, sinking air in the subtropics pushes air toward the equator. At the same time, as air rises in the tropics it sucks air in behind it at ground level. Steady trade winds blow as air is simultaneously pushed away from the subtropics and drawn toward the tropics.

Trade winds blowing from north and south of the equator meet in the middle. This creates two complete circulations of air—one to the north and one to the south. These circulations are known as Hadley Cells.

The line along which the north and south trade winds meet is called the Intertropical Convergence Zone, or ITCZ. This shifts north and south through the year, bringing distinct wet and dry seasons as it passes across different areas.

trade winds Steady winds blowing toward the equator that got their name when sailing ships carrying trade relied upon them.

cells Circulations of air in the atmosphere, with columns of rising and sinking air linked in a loop by winds at high level and on the surface.

Trade winds are mostly steady and gentle, but sometimes they can give rise to hurricanes and typhoons, the deadliest storms of all. Each summer in the Atlantic, hurricane after hurricane is born where the northeast trade winds blow down over the warm ocean off the coast of Africa.

COLLIDING TRADE WINDS

Trade winds from north and south meet at an angle along the equator outside the hurricane season

The spin of the Earth is counterclockwise

Intertropical Convergence Zone

HURRICANE TWISTER

When they meet along the equator, trade winds from the north and south meet at an angle. But in the hurricane season, they meet much farther north. The southern winds bend as they cross north over the equator and so confront the northern winds head-on—and hurricanes are born. Like a pencil twisted between two hands, the Atlantic thunderclouds are rotated between oncoming trade winds.

In late summer, the tropical sun beats down so strongly on the ocean surface that vast amounts of water turn to steam. Huge clouds then build up—each of which could become a thundercloud. For a while, they remain separate and unthreatening. To develop into a hurricane, a few extra factors are needed.

One factor comes from high-level winds blowing westward out from the African coast and over the top of the clouds. The winds usually flow at different speeds or directions from the rising air, and they break up the clouds. But every now and then the winds match closely in speed and direction, and then a storm begins to develop.

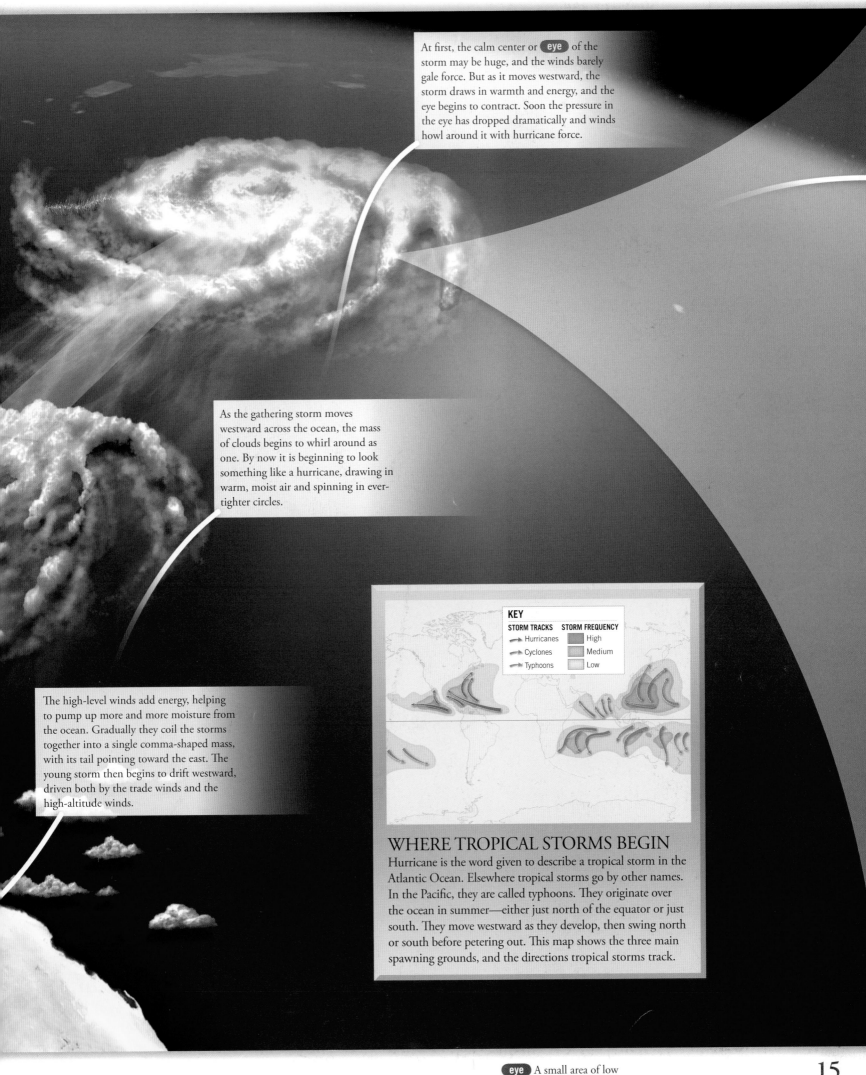

At first, the calm center or **eye** of the storm may be huge, and the winds barely gale force. But as it moves westward, the storm draws in warmth and energy, and the eye begins to contract. Soon the pressure in the eye has dropped dramatically and winds howl around it with hurricane force.

As the gathering storm moves westward across the ocean, the mass of clouds begins to whirl around as one. By now it is beginning to look something like a hurricane, drawing in warm, moist air and spinning in ever-tighter circles.

The high-level winds add energy, helping to pump up more and more moisture from the ocean. Gradually they coil the storms together into a single comma-shaped mass, with its tail pointing toward the east. The young storm then begins to drift westward, driven both by the trade winds and the high-altitude winds.

KEY

STORM TRACKS	STORM FREQUENCY
Hurricanes	High
Cyclones	Medium
Typhoons	Low

WHERE TROPICAL STORMS BEGIN

Hurricane is the word given to describe a tropical storm in the Atlantic Ocean. Elsewhere tropical storms go by other names. In the Pacific, they are called typhoons. They originate over the ocean in summer—either just north of the equator or just south. They move westward as they develop, then swing north or south before petering out. This map shows the three main spawning grounds, and the directions tropical storms track.

eye A small area of low pressure and calm in the center of a hurricane.

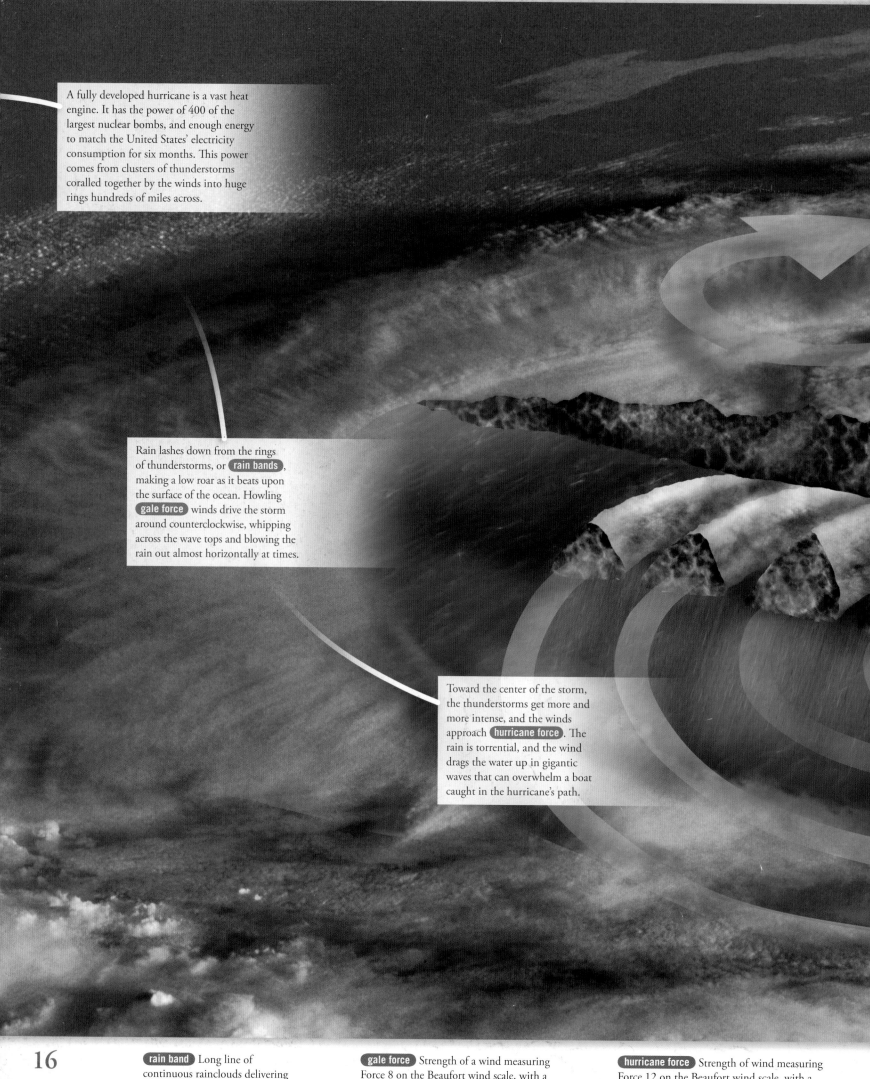

A fully developed hurricane is a vast heat engine. It has the power of 400 of the largest nuclear bombs, and enough energy to match the United States' electricity consumption for six months. This power comes from clusters of thunderstorms corralled together by the winds into huge rings hundreds of miles across.

Rain lashes down from the rings of thunderstorms, or **rain bands**, making a low roar as it beats upon the surface of the ocean. Howling **gale force** winds drive the storm around counterclockwise, whipping across the wave tops and blowing the rain out almost horizontally at times.

Toward the center of the storm, the thunderstorms get more and more intense, and the winds approach **hurricane force**. The rain is torrential, and the wind drags the water up in gigantic waves that can overwhelm a boat caught in the hurricane's path.

rain band Long line of continuous rainclouds delivering heavy rain in a hurricane.

gale force Strength of a wind measuring Force 8 on the Beaufort wind scale, with a speed of 39–46 mph (63–75 kph).

hurricane force Strength of wind measuring Force 12 on the Beaufort wind scale, with a speed of more than 73 mph (117 kph).

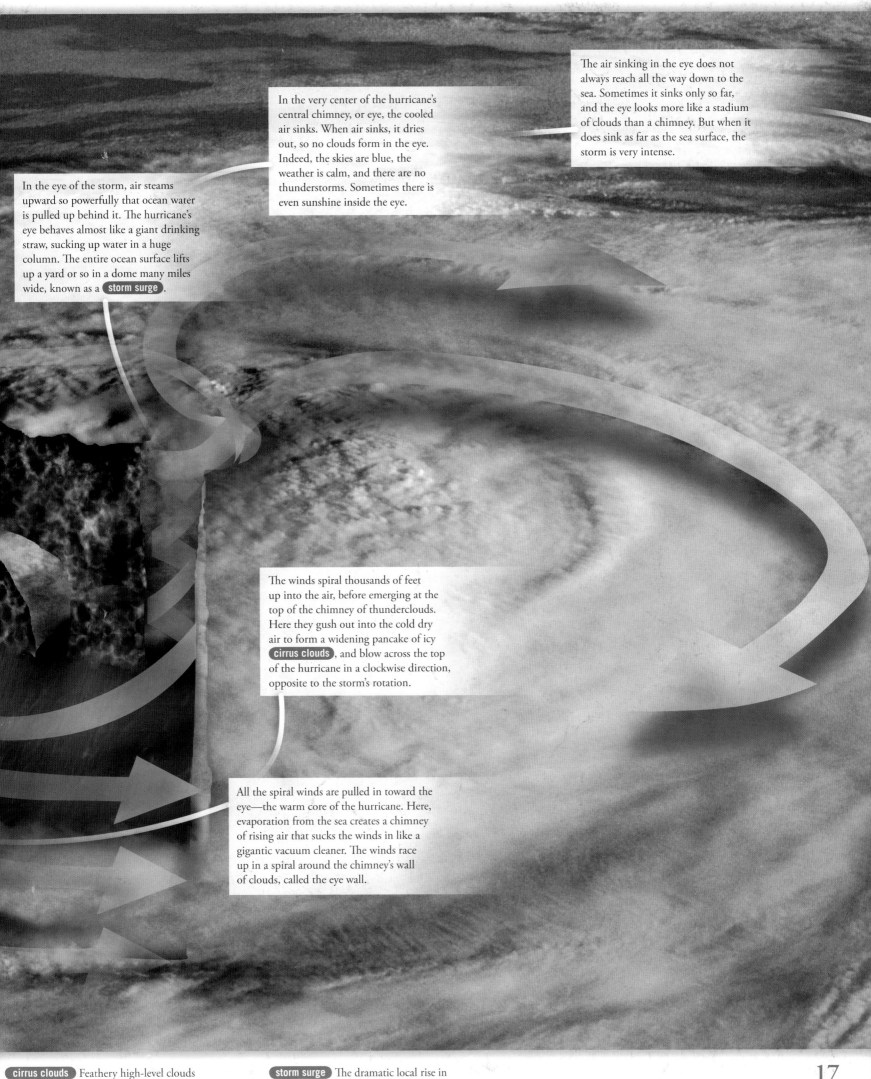

In the eye of the storm, air steams upward so powerfully that ocean water is pulled up behind it. The hurricane's eye behaves almost like a giant drinking straw, sucking up water in a huge column. The entire ocean surface lifts up a yard or so in a dome many miles wide, known as a **storm surge**.

In the very center of the hurricane's central chimney, or eye, the cooled air sinks. When air sinks, it dries out, so no clouds form in the eye. Indeed, the skies are blue, the weather is calm, and there are no thunderstorms. Sometimes there is even sunshine inside the eye.

The air sinking in the eye does not always reach all the way down to the sea. Sometimes it sinks only so far, and the eye looks more like a stadium of clouds than a chimney. But when it does sink as far as the sea surface, the storm is very intense.

The winds spiral thousands of feet up into the air, before emerging at the top of the chimney of thunderclouds. Here they gush out into the cold dry air to form a widening pancake of icy **cirrus clouds**, and blow across the top of the hurricane in a clockwise direction, opposite to the storm's rotation.

All the spiral winds are pulled in toward the eye—the warm core of the hurricane. Here, evaporation from the sea creates a chimney of rising air that sucks the winds in like a gigantic vacuum cleaner. The winds race up in a spiral around the chimney's wall of clouds, called the eye wall.

cirrus clouds Feathery high-level clouds made entirely of tiny ice crystals and typically forming more than 24,000 ft (7,300 m) up.

storm surge The dramatic local rise in sea level caused by a hurricane.

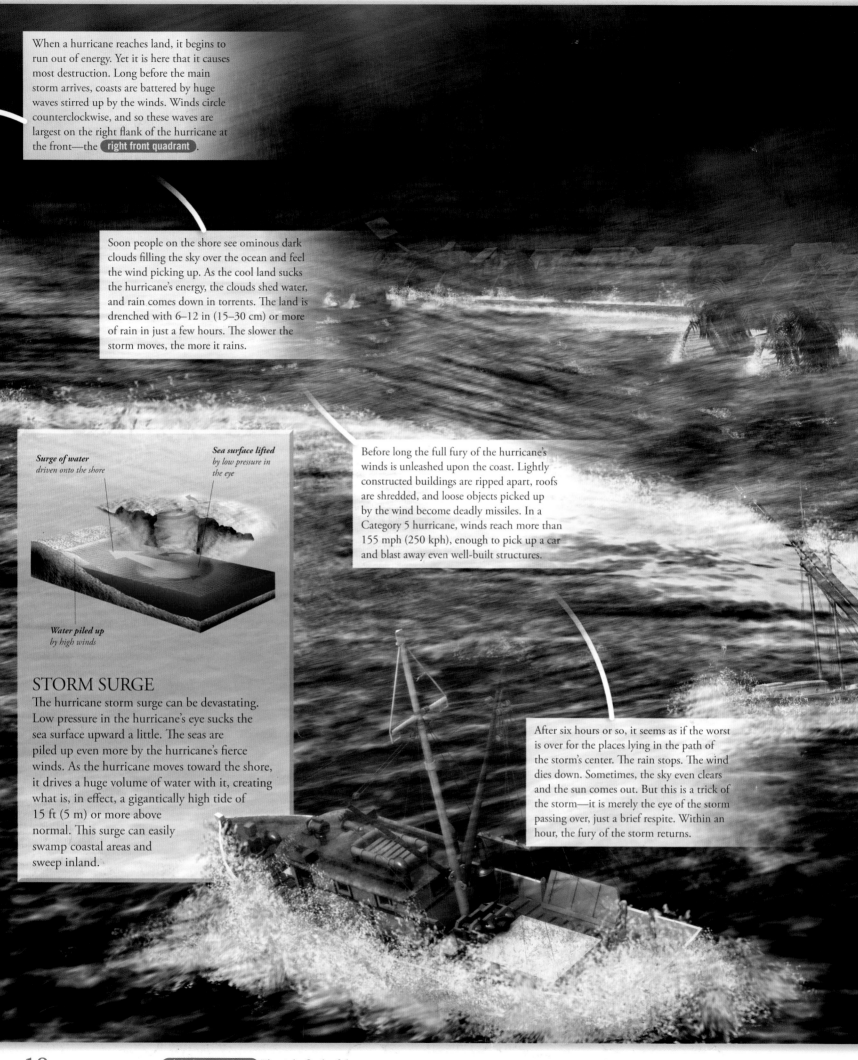

When a hurricane reaches land, it begins to run out of energy. Yet it is here that it causes most destruction. Long before the main storm arrives, coasts are battered by huge waves stirred up by the winds. Winds circle counterclockwise, and so these waves are largest on the right flank of the hurricane at the front—the **right front quadrant**.

Soon people on the shore see ominous dark clouds filling the sky over the ocean and feel the wind picking up. As the cool land sucks the hurricane's energy, the clouds shed water, and rain comes down in torrents. The land is drenched with 6–12 in (15–30 cm) or more of rain in just a few hours. The slower the storm moves, the more it rains.

Before long the full fury of the hurricane's winds is unleashed upon the coast. Lightly constructed buildings are ripped apart, roofs are shredded, and loose objects picked up by the wind become deadly missiles. In a Category 5 hurricane, winds reach more than 155 mph (250 kph), enough to pick up a car and blast away even well-built structures.

Surge of water
driven onto the shore

Sea surface lifted
by low pressure in
the eye

Water piled up
by high winds

STORM SURGE

The hurricane storm surge can be devastating. Low pressure in the hurricane's eye sucks the sea surface upward a little. The seas are piled up even more by the hurricane's fierce winds. As the hurricane moves toward the shore, it drives a huge volume of water with it, creating what is, in effect, a gigantically high tide of 15 ft (5 m) or more above normal. This surge can easily swamp coastal areas and sweep inland.

After six hours or so, it seems as if the worst is over for the places lying in the path of the storm's center. The rain stops. The wind dies down. Sometimes, the sky even clears and the sun comes out. But this is a trick of the storm—it is merely the eye of the storm passing over, just a brief respite. Within an hour, the fury of the storm returns.

right front quadrant The right flank of the hurricane, where winds blow onto the shore. A hurricane is divided into four quadrants.

For a while, the rain and wind lash the coast with relentless ferocity, but now it is the rear of the storm that is crossing. The wind **backs** around to the opposite direction, and blows from the west, not from the east, as earlier. After 12 hours or so, the rain and wind die down, and the sea recedes and begins to calm.

Storm warnings mean that people on the coast usually manage to evacuate before the surge arrives. But anything they leave behind is at the mercy of the storm. Entire beaches are washed away, even the most solid buildings are pulverized, and vehicles are swept great distances.

As the storm pushes on against the shore, the surge of water beneath the eye piles up in the coastal shallows. A gigantic tide of water overwhelms the coast, and storm waves driven by the howling winds add to the general devastation.

PREDICTING SURGES

People living near the coast need to know how big the storm surge could be. An intense storm with a low pressure eye will generate a big surge, especially if winds are strong and the hurricane is moving rapidly. But it depends, too, on the shape of the coast and the angle at which the hurricane strikes. A surge overwhelms a shallow coast far more easily than a steep coast. To predict the size of the surge, observers feed all data into the **SLOSH** computer as the hurricane approaches.

SHALLOW COAST
— *Wind waves*
— *Sea raised by storm surge*
— *Normal high tide*

STEEP COAST
— *Wind waves*
— *Sea raised by storm surge*
— *Normal high tide*

backs Wind changing in a counterclockwise direction. (A wind changing in a clockwise direction is said to veer.)

SLOSH The Sea, Lake, and Overland Surges from Hurricanes is a US computer program designed to predict storm surges.

As the storm surge retreats and the worst of the hurricane passes, the winds finally die down and the rains stop. Then, 36 hours after the hurricane hit the coast, the sun comes out and the skies clear, leaving a mass of cirrus clouds moving away into the distance.

Yet though the storm has passed, it has left a trail of destruction in its wake. Everywhere, there are uprooted trees, wrecked buildings, and collapsed power lines. The air is filled with the stench of rotting vegetation and muck dredged up by the storm surge.

When a hurricane moves slowly it may drop as much as 30 in (760 mm) or more of rain. With this amount of water draining into the river system, the flood waters may go on rising for many days before finally subsiding.

There is worse to come. Although hurricanes unleash their greatest force upon the coast, it is often inland that they claim the most lives. For days after the hurricane, rivers filled to bursting by the torrential rains begin to flood over the land to devastating effect.

For those people lucky enough to get away before the hurricane struck, it is often weeks before they can get back to their homes. When they do, it is as if their once neat neighborhood has been turned to a gigantic, festering garbage dump.

Many houses have lost their roofs to the wind. Every exposed surface has been battered by flying debris such as branches, road signs, and roof tiles. Where windows and doors have been ripped from their openings, rain and wind have lashed buildings inside and out.

Roads, power lines, and all the other essentials of a neighborhood are often completely destroyed and will take months to repair. Hurricane Andrew caused damage worth more than $15.5 billion when it struck Florida in 1992.

THE SAFFIR-SIMPSON SCALE

As hurricanes approach, hurricane watchers in the US assess each storm with an intensity rating on the Saffir-Simpson scale. This gives people an idea of the damage they might expect.

Category One
Winds of 74–95 mph (119–153 kph); storm surge of 4–5 ft (1.2–1.5 m); coastal flooding; mobile homes shaken; shrubs and road signs may be knocked over, but sturdy buildings are undamaged.

Category Two
Winds of 96–110 mph (154–178 kph); storm surge of 6–8 ft (1.8–2.4 m); heavy coastal flooding; roofs and doors damaged; mobile homes ruined; small trees uprooted.

Category Three
Winds of 111–130 mph (178–209 kph); storm surge of 9–12 ft (2.7–3.6 m); small buildings washed away; sheds and free-standing walls blown down; mobile homes rolled; large trees stripped and uprooted; structures damaged by floating debris.

Category Four
Winds of 131–155 mph (210–249 kph); storm surge of 13–18 ft (4–5.5 m); roofs blown away on homes; shrubs, trees, and signs flattened; mobile homes destroyed; roads cut off; large scale flooding.

Category Five
Winds of more than 155 mph (249 kph); storm surge more than 18 ft (5.5 m); almost complete destruction; large public and industrial buildings badly damaged; homes flattened; shrubs, trees, and signs ripped down and blown away; mobile homes destroyed; roads cut off; devastating flooding.

HURRICANE KATRINA

AUGUST 23–31, 2005

Hurricane Katrina is seen here developing in the Gulf of Mexico. The particularly warm waters supplied the energy for the hurricane to intensify rapidly into a Category 5 storm.

Hurricane Katrina was one of the deadliest and most costly natural disasters ever to hit the United States. More than 1,800 people died, and estimates place the cost of the damage at more than $100 billion. Cities such as New Orleans, which lay in the hurricane's path, may never fully recover.

Disaster area

New Orleans, Louisiana, was a thriving city of 454,000 people. During the hurricane, it was almost entirely evacuated, as 80 percent of the city was flooded. A year later, just 190,000 people had returned, and the city remained a ghost town. Cities such as Biloxi in nearby Mississippi were also ravaged. Overall, Katrina left a disaster zone of more than 90,000 sq miles (145,000 sq km) where almost half a million people lost their homes.

Katrina was one of only four Category 5 hurricanes ever known in the US. A Category 5 has winds greater than 155 mph (249 kph). But the winds of Katrina exceeded 175 mph (281 kph). Its massive storm surge of 16–30 ft (5–9 m) was the highest ever recorded in the US.

The storm is born

The storm began as a depression over the Bahamas on August 23, 2005. Hurricane watchers named it Katrina as it gained power and whirled toward Florida. It hit land on August 25 and weakened

Before and after: the dark areas in the lower picture show just how much of the city of New Orleans was flooded by the waters that breached the levées, often to a depth of 16 ft (5 m) or more.

The New Orleans Superdome became a place of refuge for thousands of people who couldn't flee the hurricane.

"It came in so fast... the house was shaking in the wind, blowing like a freight train. Our lives were in the air."

New Orleans inhabitant who stayed through the hurricane

slightly before moving out over the warm waters of the Gulf of Mexico. There it grew dramatically. On August 28, as it was upgraded to Category 5, it became clear that Katrina was heading for Mississippi and Louisiana. Warnings were issued and all along the coast people began to prepare. Roads out of New Orleans were jammed as those with cars evacuated the city. Many poor people, especially among the African American population of New Orleans, could not afford to flee. Later, there was much criticism of how little help they received.

Katrina strikes

When Katrina hit land again on August 29, Gulf Coast cities were lashed with rain and ferocious winds. The worst damage, though, was done by the storm surge. On August 30, New Orleans' levées (banks designed to protect from floods) were breached and water poured across the city. The following day, Katrina ran out of steam, but the flooding ensured that it continued to cause devastation long afterward. Conditions in New Orleans deteriorated rapidly, and the sports Superdome, the city's best available shelter, became

Huge traffic jams developed as thousands of residents returned to New Orleans after the hurricane.

In the aftermath of Katrina, a man makes his way through flood waters in the seventh ward of New Orleans as a home behind him burns. The flood waters mixed with human waste and chemicals to become a toxic brew.

a miserable place after water and power failed and desperation drove some to looting. Help was slow in coming, and President Bush was criticized for the inadequate response. Eventually, the levées were repaired, and the water pumped out. Slowly, some people returned to pick up the pieces, while others gave up hope of ever recovering what they'd lost.

National guardsmen went in search of bodies and survivors. They also had to maintain order and try to protect homes from looters.

TORNADO SEEDS

No wind storm is more terrifying than a tornado. A single tornado lasts no longer than an hour at most, but leaves in its wake a trail of utter devastation. Its awesome power begins harmlessly enough, with the morning summer sun warming the Great Plains that stretch across the heart of the United States.

SPOUTS AND DEVILS

There is a whole range of tornado types, and the supercell type described here is simply the most ferocious. When a tornado forms at sea, it forms a waterspout—a spiraling funnel that sucks up water from the sea. Dust devils in the desert form in a different way— from columns of hot air whirling up from the ground. Like waterspouts, they are less violent than supercell tornadoes, but last much longer.

The trouble begins as winds blowing around the cloud tweak and twist the **updraft**. Soon the rising warm air is spiraling, turning the giant cloud around like a mini hurricane. As the winds drive this whirling cloud toward the northwest, rain buckets down beneath its front.

Throughout the morning, the sun pumps heat into the ground, and the heated ground slowly warms the air above it. As the air warms, it expands and gets lighter. Bubbles of warm, light air drift up like balloons, carrying with them moisture that condenses into water drops as it hits cooler air higher up.

By now warm air is rushing up through the heart of the cloud in a spinning wind tunnel called a **mesocyclone**— at speeds of up to 150 mph (240 kph). Moisture is carried up so high it turns to ice, and the updraft is so strong it holds the ice airborne as it turns into **hailstones**.

By midafternoon, all these drops of water have piled up into towering thunderclouds. Then, one of these clouds begins to grow gigantic— by feeding off neighboring thunderclouds. It is in **supercell** thunderclouds such as these that the most violent tornadoes are born.

supercell A very large powerful thundercloud with a deep rotating updraft in the middle.

updraft A rising current of air.

mesocyclone A large column of air spiraling upward in the middle of a thundercloud.

hailstones Solid, layered balls of ice that form inside thunderclouds.

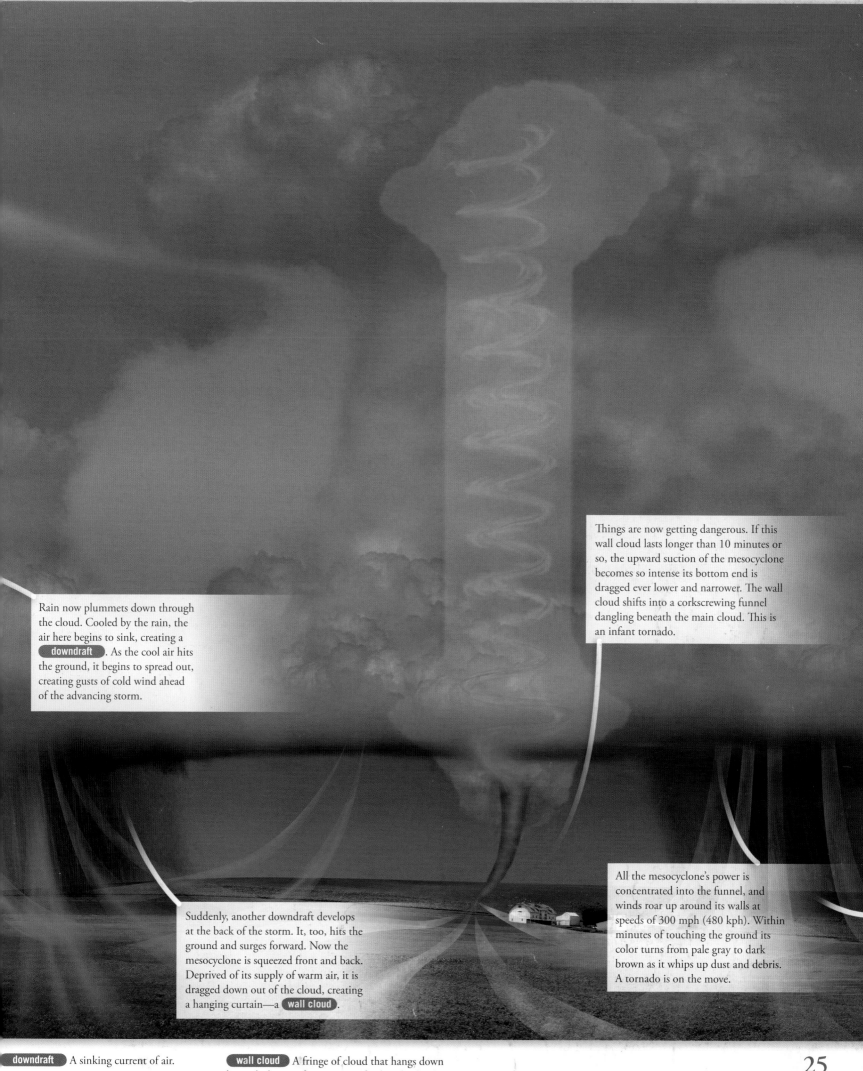

Rain now plummets down through the cloud. Cooled by the rain, the air here begins to sink, creating a **downdraft**. As the cool air hits the ground, it begins to spread out, creating gusts of cold wind ahead of the advancing storm.

Things are now getting dangerous. If this wall cloud lasts longer than 10 minutes or so, the upward suction of the mesocyclone becomes so intense its bottom end is dragged ever lower and narrower. The wall cloud shifts into a corkscrewing funnel dangling beneath the main cloud. This is an infant tornado.

Suddenly, another downdraft develops at the back of the storm. It, too, hits the ground and surges forward. Now the mesocyclone is squeezed front and back. Deprived of its supply of warm air, it is dragged down out of the cloud, creating a hanging curtain—a **wall cloud**.

All the mesocyclone's power is concentrated into the funnel, and winds roar up around its walls at speeds of 300 mph (480 kph). Within minutes of touching the ground its color turns from pale gray to dark brown as it whips up dust and debris. A tornado is on the move.

downdraft A sinking current of air.

wall cloud A fringe of cloud that hangs down beneath the rain-free portion of a thundercloud where the updraft is at its strongest.

Although it is small, the tornado is immensely powerful. Soon, the freight-train roar of its spiraling winds can be heard along with thunderclaps, and lightning flashes come from the cloud above. By now the cloud is overhead and the rain is coming down in sheets. Suddenly, the tornado strikes and chaos breaks loose.

As the cloud brings the tornado ever closer, we see that the tornado itself is small. An average tornado is just 160 ft (50 m) wide. It is very local, too, traveling only about 4–5 miles (6–8 km). So to be caught in its destructive path is very bad luck.

The dark twist of the tornado hangs ominously from the storm cloud as it moves relentlessly forward—slow enough to escape by car, but too fast to run from. The wind picks up long before the tornado arrives, as air is drawn into its hungry vortex by the low pressure.

26 **vortex** A tight, spiraling mass of gas or water that sucks everything in. **low pressure** When air pressure is low, because the air is warm, light, and rising. **lightning** A flash of natural electricity created by the buildup of electrical charge inside a churning thundercloud.

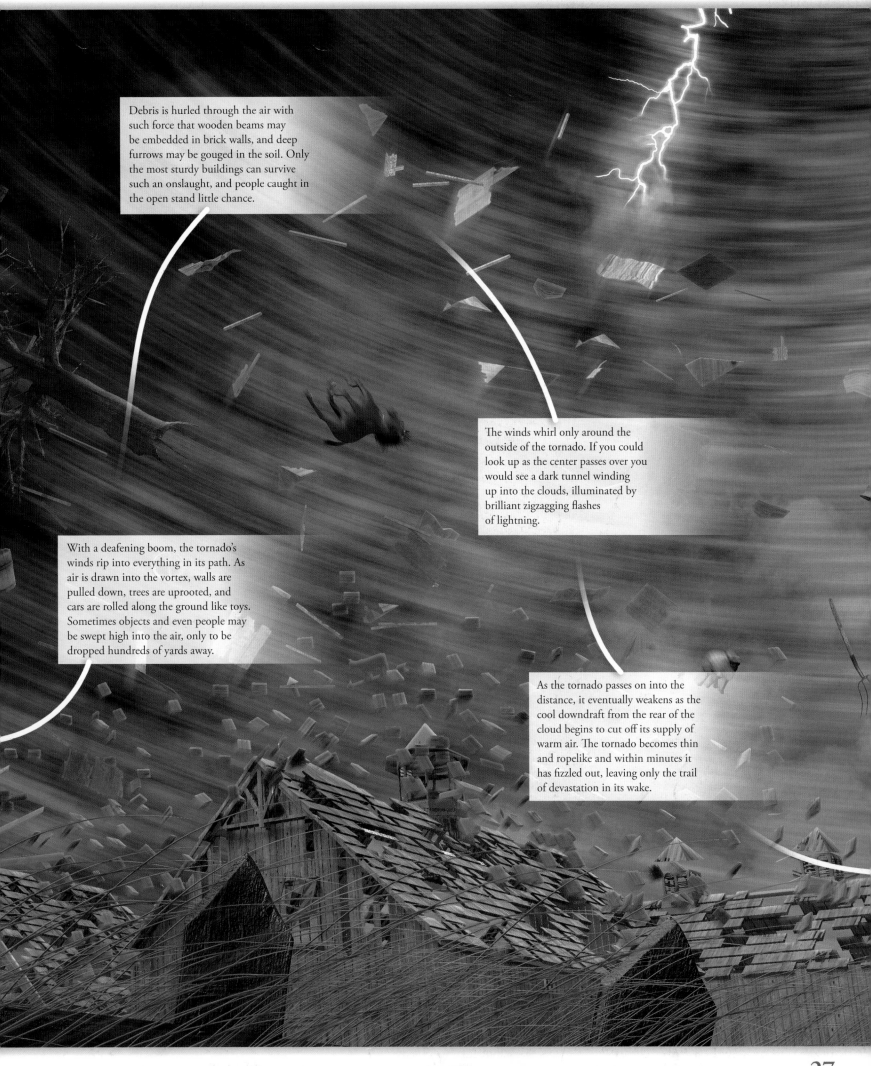

Debris is hurled through the air with such force that wooden beams may be embedded in brick walls, and deep furrows may be gouged in the soil. Only the most sturdy buildings can survive such an onslaught, and people caught in the open stand little chance.

The winds whirl only around the outside of the tornado. If you could look up as the center passes over you would see a dark tunnel winding up into the clouds, illuminated by brilliant zigzagging flashes of lightning.

With a deafening boom, the tornado's winds rip into everything in its path. As air is drawn into the vortex, walls are pulled down, trees are uprooted, and cars are rolled along the ground like toys. Sometimes objects and even people may be swept high into the air, only to be dropped hundreds of yards away.

As the tornado passes on into the distance, it eventually weakens as the cool downdraft from the rear of the cloud begins to cut off its supply of warm air. The tornado becomes thin and ropelike and within minutes it has fizzled out, leaving only the trail of devastation in its wake.

Many houses in the tornado's path have exploded. Air pressure inside the houses was normal, but the pressure within the vortex was so low that when it passed over the house the air inside expanded, blowing the house apart.

If any twisters are spotted on Doppler radar, a tornado warning is issued. This is very important. Few forces of nature destroy people's lives so utterly in so little time. The damage is done mostly by fearsome winds of up to 300 mph (480 kph).

Wherever they strike, twisters bring devastation. Most are over in just a few minutes, with a brief touchdown that leaves a trail barely 160 ft (50 m) wide and less than 1 mile (2 km) long. But the awesome power of the vortex wreaks havoc on anything or anyone in its path.

28

twisters A slang term for tornadoes. The name comes from the twisting shape of the tornado's vortex.

touchdown When a tornado's vortex snakes down from a cloud and touches the ground.

Doppler radar A forecasting device that sends out radio waves and uses the reflections to detect rainfall.

tornado warning Alert sent out when a tornado is spotted on Doppler radar.

The vortex is often only as wide as a single house and yard. So it may destroy one house while leaving the one next door virtually unscratched. This is particularly so when the tornado consisted of lots of small vortices, known as subvortices.

Objects as heavy as cows and cars may have been picked up by the wind and dropped as much as a mile away. Lighter objects such as letters, pictures, and even panes of glass may be carried up to 50 miles (80 km). People, too, may have been carried into the air if they were caught in the vortex.

Some of the damage is caused by objects hurled in the ferocious tornado winds. Flying debris may strike solid buildings with the force of bullets. Loose stones or bricks blown against a wall may knock it down.

THE FUJITA SCALE

In the United States the damage done by a tornado is often measured on a scale devised by Chicago tornado expert Theodore Fujita.

F0 Gale Tornado wind speed: 40–72 mph (65–116 kph); some damage to chimneys; breaks branches off trees; pushes over shallow-rooted trees; damages signposts.

F1 Moderate Tornado wind speed: 73–112 mph (117–180 kph); roofs damaged; mobile homes blown over; cars blown off roads.

F2 Significant Tornado wind speed: 113–157 mph (181–250 kph); roofs torn off houses; mobile homes demolished; vans pushed over; large trees snapped or uprooted.

F3 Severe Tornado wind speed: 158–206 mph (251–330 kph); roof and some walls torn off well-built houses; trains overturned; most trees in forests uprooted.

F4 Devastating Tornado wind speed: 207–260 mph (331–415 kph); houses flattened; lighter buildings blown away; cars thrown.

F5 Incredible Tornado wind speed: 261–318 mph (416–510 kph); strong frame houses lifted; cars carried away; trees stripped of bark; steel reinforced concrete structures badly damaged.

Tornado winds can bend over trees and crack them open, then blow debris such as straw or even old records into the cracks. After the tornado passes, the tree straightens, the crack snaps shut, and the object is firmly trapped in the tree.

subvortices Mini vortexes inside the main tornado vortex that leave distinctive spiral markings on the ground.

TRI-STATE TWISTER

MARCH 18, 1925

The Tri-State Twister was one of the worst storms in recorded history. It was certainly the most devastating ever known in the United States. In just a few hours on March 18, 1925, it ripped through the states of Missouri, Illinois, and Indiana, moving at a speed of 73 mph (117 kph). In its wake four towns were left utterly destroyed, six towns badly damaged, 15,000 homes wrecked, 2,000 people injured and 695 people dead. Even today, the region is haunted by the ghost towns left by the twister.

After the tornado, *survivors search for bodies amid the wreckage of Griffin, Indiana, where 25 people died.*

The vortex descends

The morning of March 18 was clear and gave no inkling of what was to come. This was in the days before tornado warning systems. Soon after 1 p.m., a thunderstorm erupted and people near Ellington, Missouri, saw a vortex descending from a cloud. From there on, the tornado moved northeast at incredible speed. For the next 3.5 hours—the longest lifespan of any tornado—the giant vortex cut a swathe of destruction 219 miles (353 km) long across the Midwest.

Trail of devastation

Within 15 minutes, the little town of Annapolis, Missouri, was reduced almost to rubble and two people lost their lives.

> "Then the wind struck the school. The walls seemed to fall in all around us. Then the floor one end of the building gave way..."
>
> *Schoolgirl in Gorham, Illinois*

The Tri-State *was a tornado like this one—only far bigger and more powerful than nearly any other recorded. Measuring F5 on the Fujita scale, Incredible Tornado, it was at times almost 1 mile (1.6 km) wide, with winds racing around it at over 300 mph (nearly 500 kph)!*

But far worse was to come as the tornado raced east. Over much of Missouri its path was across farmland. But as it crossed into southern Illinois, the towns of Gorham, Murphysboro, De Soto, and West Frankfort found themselves directly in the tornado's path. Gorham was first to be hit, at 2:26 p.m. Within a few minutes, this thriving town was devastated, with 34 of its inhabitants dead. Just eight minutes later, Murphysboro was gone too, with 234 people dead. A minute after that De Soto was destroyed. Within another four minutes the tornado was upon West Frankfort.

The miners' tragedy

West Frankfort was a mining town. When the tornado struck, many of the town's men were deep underground in the pit. All they knew of the storm was that it had cut the electrical power, and with it the elevators. The miners climbed

In most towns, not a building was left standing. Not a tree was left with its branches. Here, a relief effort is being mounted to feed and clothe one town's survivors.

---

strenuously up an emergency shaft. When they emerged onto the surface, they were met by a scene of utter destruction. The homes they had left just hours earlier were destroyed, and many wives and children, girlfriends, and mothers had perished.

The monster vanishes

By the time the storm passed out of Illinois and into Indiana at 4 p.m, 613 people were dead. Yet it was still not finished. Crossing the Wabash River, it wiped out the town of Griffin, wrecked Owensville, then tore into Princeton,

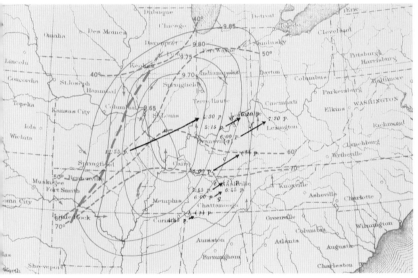

The mighty storm traveled farther than any tornado in history, cutting a path of destruction 1–1.5 miles (0.6–1 km) wide across three states, earning it the name Tri-State Twister. The general path of the storm is shown by the long black lines on the map.

Tossed aside like a tent, this solidly built farmhouse was ripped from its foundations and blown into a clump of trees.

destroying half the town. Finally, at 4:30 p.m the vortex vanished back into the cloud and the monster was gone.

For those who survived, it had been a terrible experience. Afterward, one Gorham schoolgirl described it like this: "Then the air was filled with 10,000 things. Boards, poles, cans, garments, stoves, whole sides of the little frame houses—in some cases the houses themselves—were picked up and smashed to earth. And living beings, too. A baby was blown from its mother's arms. A cow, picked up by the wind, was hurled into the village restaurant."

This solid brick school in Murphysboro, Illinois, was one of many schools destroyed by the tornado, which killed more children than any other tornado in history.

THE FOGGIEST PLACE

For more than 120 days each year, the sea off the coast of Newfoundland in Canada is shrouded in **fog**. Here, again and again in late spring and summer, a thick, silvery fog creeps silently over the Atlantic waters. Fog is made from tiny droplets of moisture floating in the air. Individually the droplets are too small to see, but together they form a dense cloak of invisibility.

The fog begins with a **gentle breeze** blowing in from the southwest. The breeze needs to be strong enough to bring in moist air to form the fog, but not so strong that it would blow the fog away as swiftly as it formed. Wind is usually about 10–15 mph (17–24 kph).

The southwesterly breeze is warm, because it comes from the sunny south. In addition, it has wafted over the warm waters of the **Gulf Stream** — the ocean current that flows all the way up the east coast of North America from the Gulf of Mexico.

Warm air is like a sponge, and can soak up huge amounts of moisture invisibly. So on its journey over the Gulf Stream, the southwesterly breeze has become laden with moisture evaporated from the water. The air is still completely clear, though, because in warm air the moisture turns to invisible vapor.

Off the eastern point of Newfoundland, something dramatic happens. While the warm Gulf Stream is flowing north along Newfoundland's southern coast, a much colder current is driving south along Newfoundland's northern coast. This is the icy **Labrador Current**, streaming down from the Arctic Ocean.

fog A cloud that forms at the surface and restricts visibility to less than 3,300 ft (1,000 m) at sea and 660 ft (200 m) on land.

gentle breeze A light wind measuring Force 3 on the Beaufort wind scale, with a speed of 8–12 mph (13–19 kph).

Gulf Stream A warm Atlantic current that starts in the Gulf of Mexico and crosses to Europe, where it becomes the North Atlantic Drift.

As the breeze brings in more moist air, the fog thickens until the coast, shipping, and everything in the coastal waters is hidden in its soft blanket. Here, off Newfoundland, fog may persist for weeks before the wind changes direction or becomes stronger and blows it away.

Cool air holds much less moisture than warm air. So, as the air is chilled, the moisture it contains condenses into tiny droplets of water. These water drops are so tiny that they float on the air, and as they do they create a white fog.

As it blows out beyond Newfoundland's easterly tip, the warm, moist, southwesterly breeze suddenly begins to cross the cold Labrador Current instead of the Gulf Stream. Instantly, the lower layers of the air are chilled by the cold water.

DEADLY ICEBERGS

Every now and then, chunks of ice break off from the Arctic ice sheet and are swept south by the Labrador Current. Here, they present a major danger to ships. Undetectable on radar, these shifting chunks are worrying enough in clear weather. But when they are hidden by fog, icebergs are lurking menaces to ships. Most famously, the passenger ship *Titanic* collided with one at night in April 1912 and sank, killing 1,523 people.

Labrador Current A cold current in the north Atlantic Ocean that flows south from the Arctic Ocean and past Newfoundland.

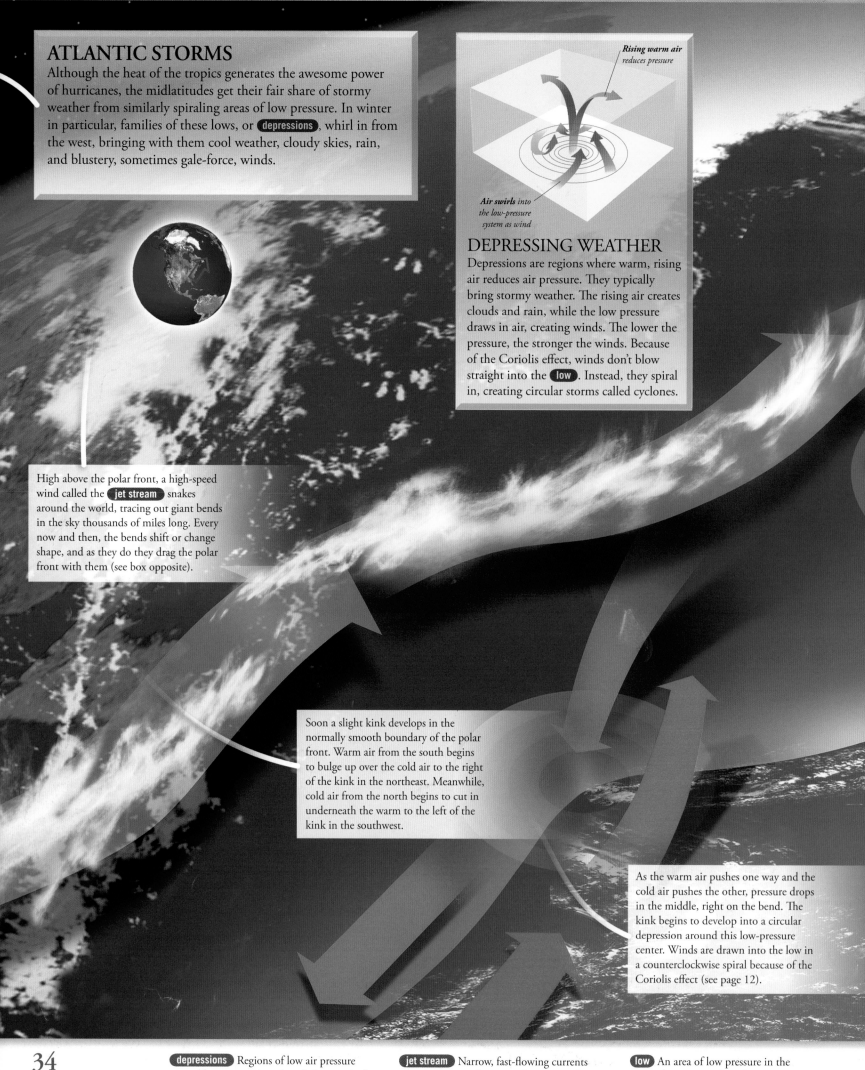

ATLANTIC STORMS

Although the heat of the tropics generates the awesome power of hurricanes, the midlatitudes get their fair share of stormy weather from similarly spiraling areas of low pressure. In winter in particular, families of these lows, or **depressions**, whirl in from the west, bringing with them cool weather, cloudy skies, rain, and blustery, sometimes gale-force, winds.

Rising warm air reduces pressure

Air swirls into the low-pressure system as wind

DEPRESSING WEATHER

Depressions are regions where warm, rising air reduces air pressure. They typically bring stormy weather. The rising air creates clouds and rain, while the low pressure draws in air, creating winds. The lower the pressure, the stronger the winds. Because of the Coriolis effect, winds don't blow straight into the **low**. Instead, they spiral in, creating circular storms called cyclones.

High above the polar front, a high-speed wind called the **jet stream** snakes around the world, tracing out giant bends in the sky thousands of miles long. Every now and then, the bends shift or change shape, and as they do they drag the polar front with them (see box opposite).

Soon a slight kink develops in the normally smooth boundary of the polar front. Warm air from the south begins to bulge up over the cold air to the right of the kink in the northeast. Meanwhile, cold air from the north begins to cut in underneath the warm to the left of the kink in the southwest.

As the warm air pushes one way and the cold air pushes the other, pressure drops in the middle, right on the bend. The kink begins to develop into a circular depression around this low-pressure center. Winds are drawn into the low in a counterclockwise spiral because of the Coriolis effect (see page 12).

depressions Regions of low air pressure created by warm, rising air and characterized by stormy weather.

jet stream Narrow, fast-flowing currents of air high up in the atmosphere, typically 36,000 ft (11,000 m) up.

low An area of low pressure in the atmosphere, especially a depression.

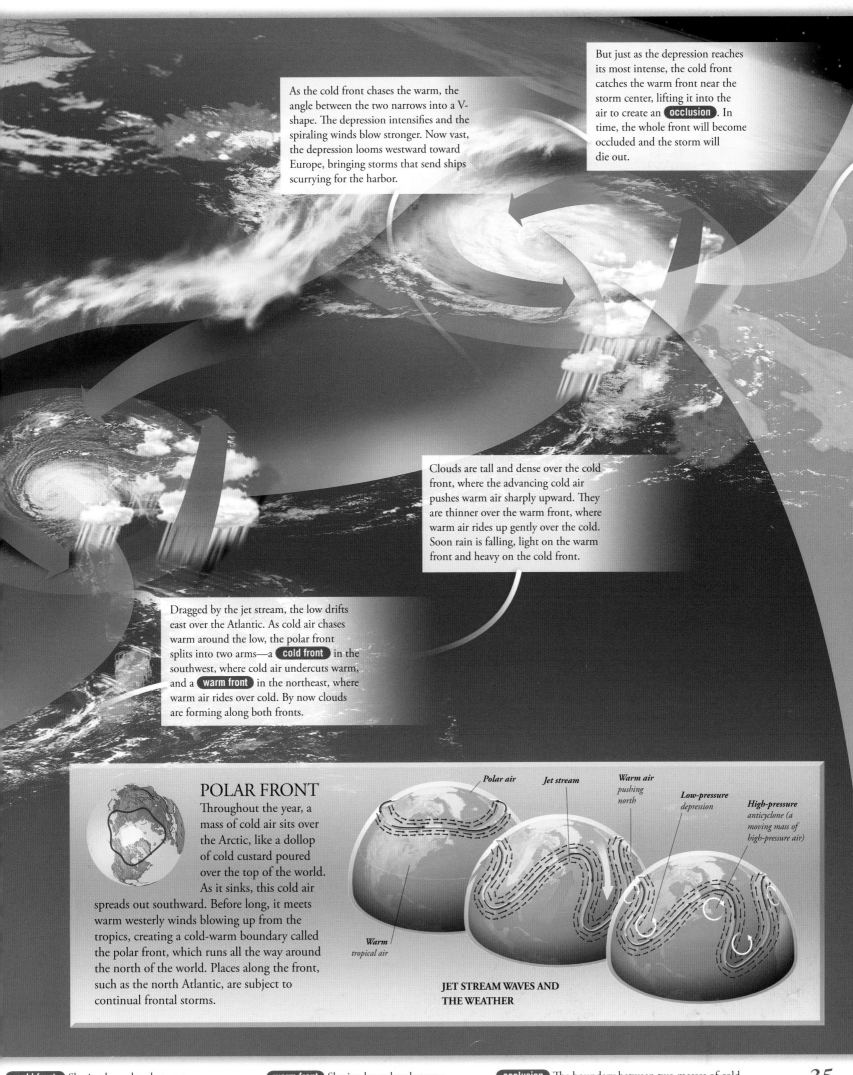

As the cold front chases the warm, the angle between the two narrows into a V-shape. The depression intensifies and the spiraling winds blow stronger. Now vast, the depression looms westward toward Europe, bringing storms that send ships scurrying for the harbor.

But just as the depression reaches its most intense, the cold front catches the warm front near the storm center, lifting it into the air to create an **occlusion**. In time, the whole front will become occluded and the storm will die out.

Clouds are tall and dense over the cold front, where the advancing cold air pushes warm air sharply upward. They are thinner over the warm front, where warm air rides up gently over the cold. Soon rain is falling, light on the warm front and heavy on the cold front.

Dragged by the jet stream, the low drifts east over the Atlantic. As cold air chases warm around the low, the polar front splits into two arms—a **cold front** in the southwest, where cold air undercuts warm, and a **warm front** in the northeast, where warm air rides over cold. By now clouds are forming along both fronts.

POLAR FRONT

Throughout the year, a mass of cold air sits over the Arctic, like a dollop of cold custard poured over the top of the world. As it sinks, this cold air spreads out southward. Before long, it meets warm westerly winds blowing up from the tropics, creating a cold-warm boundary called the polar front, which runs all the way around the north of the world. Places along the front, such as the north Atlantic, are subject to continual frontal storms.

Polar air

Jet stream

Warm air *pushing north*

Low-pressure *depression*

High-pressure *anticyclone (a moving mass of high-pressure air)*

Warm *tropical air*

JET STREAM WAVES AND THE WEATHER

cold front Sloping boundary between masses of warm air and cold air where the cold air is advancing.

warm front Sloping boundary between masses of warm air and cold air where the warm air is advancing.

occlusion The boundary between two masses of cold air that is formed when a cold front catches a warm front and lifts the wedge of warm air off the ground.

The first sign of an approaching Atlantic storm is the sight of wispy, cirrus clouds high in the sky. These clouds are made entirely of ice and form the leading edge of the warm front—the first front to arrive—as it moves steadily eastward across the landscape.

Soon, the blue sky begins to fill up with milky veils of **cirrostratus** clouds, formed lower down on the front. Within a few hours, the air pressure has started to drop, and a breeze begins to pick up. The air is noticeably chillier.

The warm front advances over the landscape, and after six hours or so has come down to just a few thousand yards above the ground. The sky is gray with **altostratus** clouds and it's getting windier.

AIR MASSES

Vast portions of the air are almost uniformly wet or dry, cold or warm, over large areas called air masses. Our weather depends largely on the air mass above us. North America, for example, is influenced by six air masses (right). Sometimes, the air mass does not move and we get the same weather for days. But a change of wind may bring the influence of a new air mass.

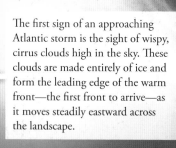

Polar Maritime (cold, damp)

Polar Continental (cold, dry)

Polar Maritime (cold, damp)

NORTH AMERICA

PACIFIC OCEAN

ATLANTIC OCEAN

Tropical continental

Tropical Maritime (warm, moist)

Tropical Maritime (warm, moist)

cirrostratus Milky, veil-like clouds of ice, typically forming 20,000–42,000 ft (6,000–13,000 m) up.

altostratus A layer of flat, featureless cloud typically forming 6,500–23,000 ft (2,000–7,000 m) up.

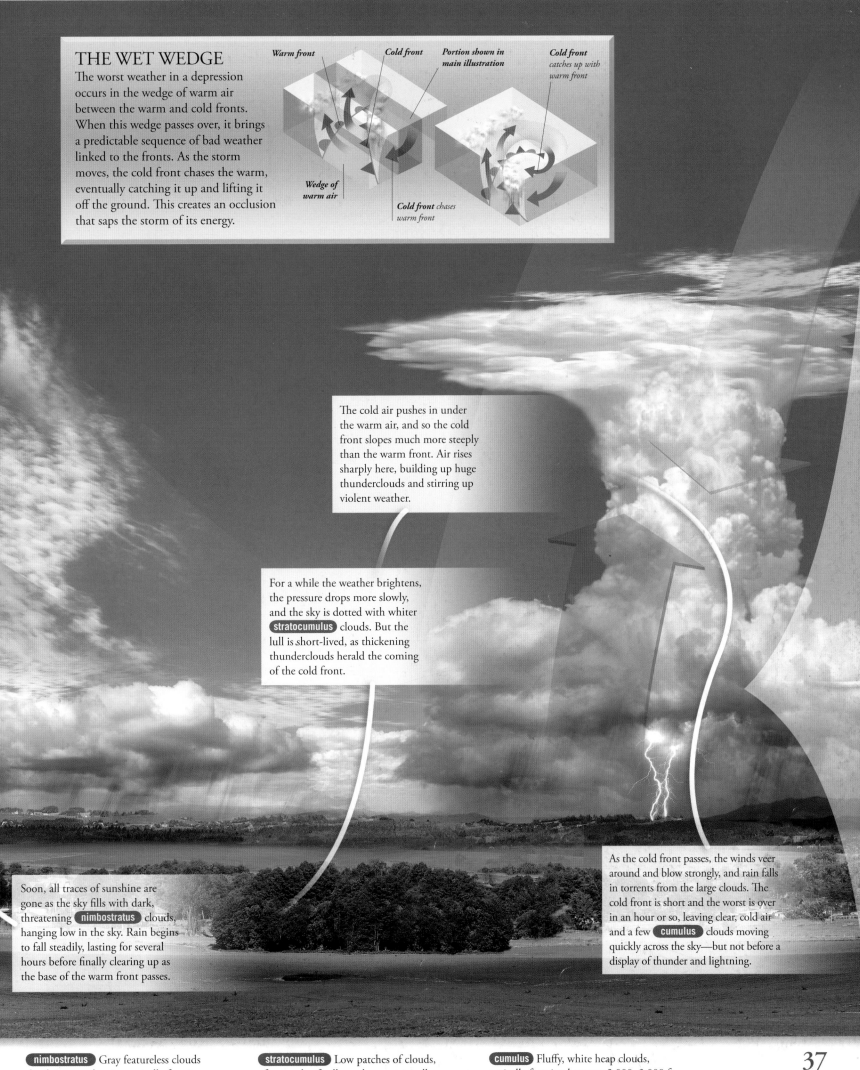

THE WET WEDGE

The worst weather in a depression occurs in the wedge of warm air between the warm and cold fronts. When this wedge passes over, it brings a predictable sequence of bad weather linked to the fronts. As the storm moves, the cold front chases the warm, eventually catching it up and lifting it off the ground. This creates an occlusion that saps the storm of its energy.

Warm front

Cold front

Portion shown in main illustration

Cold front catches up with warm front

Wedge of warm air

Cold front chases warm front

The cold air pushes in under the warm air, and so the cold front slopes much more steeply than the warm front. Air rises sharply here, building up huge thunderclouds and stirring up violent weather.

For a while the weather brightens, the pressure drops more slowly, and the sky is dotted with whiter **stratocumulus** clouds. But the lull is short-lived, as thickening thunderclouds herald the coming of the cold front.

Soon, all traces of sunshine are gone as the sky fills with dark, threatening **nimbostratus** clouds, hanging low in the sky. Rain begins to fall steadily, lasting for several hours before finally clearing up as the base of the warm front passes.

As the cold front passes, the winds veer around and blow strongly, and rain falls in torrents from the large clouds. The cold front is short and the worst is over in an hour or so, leaving clear, cold air and a few **cumulus** clouds moving quickly across the sky—but not before a display of thunder and lightning.

nimbostratus Gray featureless clouds that bring steady rain, typically forming 2,000–18,000 ft (600–5,400 m) up.

stratocumulus Low patches of clouds, often made of rolls or clumps, typically forming 2,000–6,500 ft (600–2,000 m) up.

cumulus Fluffy, white heap clouds, typically forming between 2,000–3,000 ft (600–1,000 m) up.

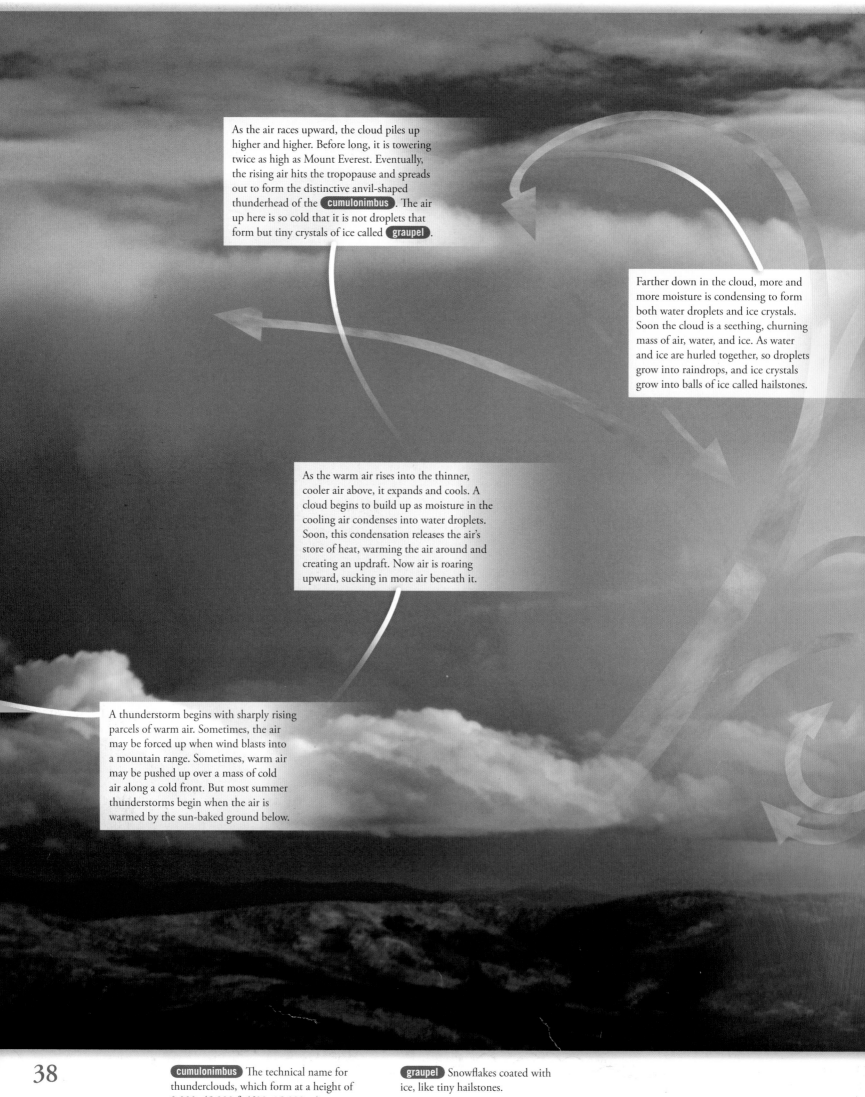

As the air races upward, the cloud piles up higher and higher. Before long, it is towering twice as high as Mount Everest. Eventually, the rising air hits the tropopause and spreads out to form the distinctive anvil-shaped thunderhead of the **cumulonimbus**. The air up here is so cold that it is not droplets that form but tiny crystals of ice called **graupel**.

Farther down in the cloud, more and more moisture is condensing to form both water droplets and ice crystals. Soon the cloud is a seething, churning mass of air, water, and ice. As water and ice are hurled together, so droplets grow into raindrops, and ice crystals grow into balls of ice called hailstones.

As the warm air rises into the thinner, cooler air above, it expands and cools. A cloud begins to build up as moisture in the cooling air condenses into water droplets. Soon, this condensation releases the air's store of heat, warming the air around and creating an updraft. Now air is roaring upward, sucking in more air beneath it.

A thunderstorm begins with sharply rising parcels of warm air. Sometimes, the air may be forced up when wind blasts into a mountain range. Sometimes, warm air may be pushed up over a mass of cold air along a cold front. But most summer thunderstorms begin when the air is warmed by the sun-baked ground below.

cumulonimbus The technical name for thunderclouds, which form at a height of 2,000–45,000 ft (600–15,000 m).

graupel Snowflakes coated with ice, like tiny hailstones.

The raindrops and hailstones are soon so heavy that the updraft can no longer hold them in the air. Then they begin to plummet, dragging the surrounding air down with them and creating a downdraft. Some even evaporate, cooling the air around still more and accelerating the downdraft to speeds of 125 mph (200 kph) or more.

HAILSTONES

Thunderclouds don't just rain down drops of water. They drop balls of solid ice called hailstones, too. These are typically as large as peas, but sometimes as large as apples. Hailstones form in thunderclouds because the clouds are so tall that the upper levels are very cold, and so turbulent that they can hold ice balls aloft. Hailstones form in the cloud's main updraft, where most water is **supercooled**. Supercooled water stays liquid until it finds something, such as an ice crystal, to freeze onto. The crystal quickly acquires more layers of ice, gets heavier and bigger, and falls from the cloud as a hailstone.

By now, rain and hail are hurtling down through the cloud. Suddenly, the downdraft blows from the base of the cloud and roars out ahead of the storm in a chilling gust of wind. This is the **gust front** that tells us the storm is on its way. High-power, concentrated **downbursts** called **microbursts** can wreak havoc.

Not far behind the downburst of wind comes the rain and hail. Torrents of water and ice are hurled to the ground, battering roofs and bringing flooding. But the storm rarely lasts more than an hour, and the dark thundercloud vanishes as quickly as it came.

gust front The windy, front-edge of the rain-cooled air that precedes a thunderstorm, like a mini cold front.

downbursts Strong, sudden, localized downdrafts.

microbursts Very localized and concentrated downdrafts.

supercooled When water stays liquid well below its freezing point—32°F (0°C).

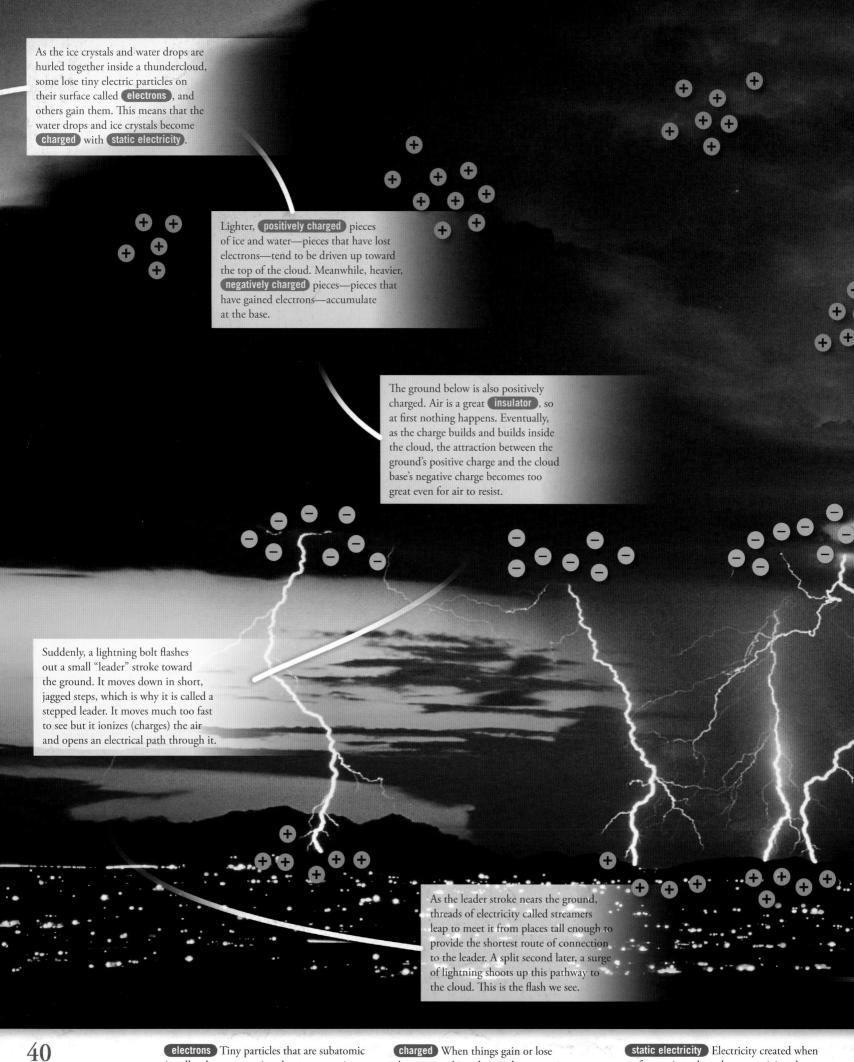

As the ice crystals and water drops are hurled together inside a thundercloud, some lose tiny electric particles on their surface called **electrons**, and others gain them. This means that the water drops and ice crystals become **charged** with **static electricity**.

Lighter, **positively charged** pieces of ice and water—pieces that have lost electrons—tend to be driven up toward the top of the cloud. Meanwhile, heavier, **negatively charged** pieces—pieces that have gained electrons—accumulate at the base.

The ground below is also positively charged. Air is a great **insulator**, so at first nothing happens. Eventually, as the charge builds and builds inside the cloud, the attraction between the ground's positive charge and the cloud base's negative charge becomes too great even for air to resist.

Suddenly, a lightning bolt flashes out a small "leader" stroke toward the ground. It moves down in short, jagged steps, which is why it is called a stepped leader. It moves much too fast to see but it ionizes (charges) the air and opens an electrical path through it.

As the leader stroke nears the ground, threads of electricity called streamers leap to meet it from places tall enough to provide the shortest route of connection to the leader. A split second later, a surge of lightning shoots up this pathway to the cloud. This is the flash we see.

40

electrons Tiny particles that are subatomic (smaller than an atom) and carry a negative electrical charge.

charged When things gain or lose electrons, making them either attractive or repulsive to other electrons.

static electricity Electricity created when surfaces gain or lose electrons, giving them a natural attraction or repulsion to each other.

SPRITES AND ELVES

Most people are familiar with just two types of lightning—fork lightning (lightning between cloud and ground) and sheet lightning (lightning within the cloud). But in the 1990s, scientists confirmed the existence of several other types of lightning—types that surge from the cloud tops and are only visible from the air. These include giant red pillars called sprites, broad disks called elves, and beams that shoot out of the cloud top called blue jets (seen here).

We only see clearly the bolts of lightning that flash between the cloud and the ground. But most lightning flashes occur within the cloud as electricity leaps between the negatively charged base and the positively charged top. These in-cloud flashes light up the cloud and are called sheet lightning.

LIGHTNING STRIKE

When a tree is hit by lightning, the intense heat vaporizes the tree's sap. As the sap vaporizes, it expands hugely, and so bursts the tree apart from the inside. Usually, lightning runs just beneath the bark so only bark is stripped away and the tree survives, scarred. Occasionally, however, the lightning runs down the center of the trunk and blows the tree completely apart.

As a lightning bolt flashes, it heats the air around to a temperature five times as hot as the Sun's surface. The heat swells the air at supersonic speed, sending out a shockwave of thunder. Sound travels slower than light, and so the sound of thunder arrives after the lightning.

positively charged A loss of electrons.   **negatively charged** A gain in electrons.   **insulator** Anything that hinders the movement of electrons.

CATALOG OF CLOUD TYPES

Clouds float across the sky in an infinite variety of shapes and forms, and are constantly changing. Yet cloud shapes are not random. They take particular shapes according to the conditions in which they form. Clouds come in three basic shapes—puffy (cumulus type), layered (stratus type), and feathery (cirrus type). They can also be classified according to the height at which they occur (low, medium, and high), and by recognizable patterns.

HIGH-LEVEL CLOUD

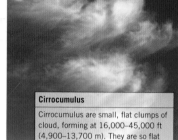

Cirrus

Cirrus are the highest of all clouds, forming at 16,000–45,000 ft (4,900–13,700 m). It is so cold at this altitude that they are made entirely of tiny crystals. Strong winds in the upper atmosphere blow them out into wisps that are said to look like horses' tails.

Cirrocumulus

Cirrocumulus are small, flat clumps of cloud, forming at 16,000–45,000 ft (4,900–13,700 m). They are so flat that they never have shadows on them, unlike altocumulus, which they can resemble. Like all cirrus-type clouds, they are made entirely of ice crystals.

Cirrostratus

Cirrostratus form where cirrus clouds spread into a wide, milky veil at 16,500–30,000 ft (5,000–9,100 m). They are faint and easy to miss, but sometimes the sun can be seen shining very brightly through them, surrounded by haloes.

MIDDLE-LEVEL CLOUD

Altostratus

Altostratus are flat clouds that can stretch across the whole sky, forming at 6,500–23,000 ft (2,000–7,000 m). They are made from water droplets and ice, and may be thin enough for the sun to glow through. They are usually dry, but may produce light rain or snow.

Altocumulus

Altocumulus are puffs of clouds forming at 6,500–18,000 ft (2,000–5,500 m). They are made mostly of water drops. Unlike flatter cirrocumulus, the deeper rolls of altocumulus have one dark side and one light because of the way sunlight catches them.

LOW-LEVEL CLOUD

Cumulus

Cumulus are the classic, cotton ball clouds, shaped like cauliflowers floating at 2,000–3,000 ft (600–900 m). These clouds form by warm currents of rising air, and usually signify fair weather. They are often brilliant white, but can turn dark when the sun is behind them.

Stratocumulus

Stratocumulus clouds are like cumulus clouds that have spread sideways and filled up the sky. They form clumps and mounds at 2,000–6,500 ft (600–2,000 m). Looking down from an aircraft, they appear as an undulating blanket of cloud rolls.

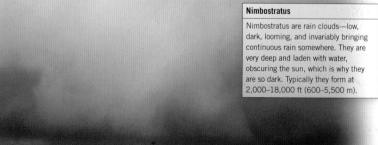

Nimbostratus

Nimbostratus are rain clouds—low, dark, looming, and invariably bringing continuous rain somewhere. They are very deep and laden with water, obscuring the sun, which is why they are so dark. Typically they form at 2,000–18,000 ft (600–5,500 m).

Stratus

Stratus clouds are vast, gray, and dull and sometimes hang so low over the ground at 0–6,500 ft (0–2,000 m) that they become fog. They may give damp drizzle every now and then, but they rarely give real rain. Clouds like these can blot out the sun for days on end.

Lenticular clouds

Lenticular clouds are among the most spectacular of all clouds. They get their name because they look like lenses. They are typically a type of altocumulus cloud and form in the lee of mountains after the air has been forced up and over the peaks.

Mammatus clouds

Mammatus get their name from the Latin for breasts, and hang from the underside of clouds like a field of cows' udders. They form as other clouds do, but in reverse—from cold air sinking through a cloud rather than from bubbles of warm rising air.

Mackerel sky

Mackerel skies are large patches of cirrocumulus clouds blown into lines of wavy ripples by strong winds high in the atmosphere. They get their name because they resemble the scales on a mackerel fish. Clouds like these are a sign of bad weather on the way.

Virga

Cirrus clouds often drop ice crystals that evaporate as they fall into drier, slower-moving air. As they fall, they form veils called virga that look like the tendrils of a jellyfish. Sometimes virga form lower in the sky and are made of evaporating raindrops.

ARCTIC CHILL

The Arctic is one of the coldest places on Earth. In summer, the Sun peeks over the top of the world here, and almost never sets. Even so, it stays so low in the sky that the weather is only cool at best. Yet now fall is coming to the Arctic and the Sun barely climbs above the horizon. By midwinter, it won't rise at all. It will be dark 24 hours a day and the temperatures may plummet to a bitter -94°F (-70°C).

The low angle of the Arctic sun means that some mountain slopes remain forever in deep, chilly shadow. Even where it is sunny, the Arctic snow is so white and shiny that it reflects away most of the Sun's warmth. So a bitter chill descends as soon as the Sun dips below the horizon.

The coldness of the air here means that it can hold very little moisture. So some places in the Arctic are drier than tropical deserts. Only briefly during fall are there clouds moving in off the sea to drop moisture in the form of snow.

Even in summer, the Arctic sun is too weak to melt much of the vast sheets of ice that cover Greenland and float on the sea around the North Pole. This permanent floating ice is called pack ice and is more than 20 ft (6 m) thick.

As the Arctic fall nights get longer and the air gets colder, the sea around the pack ice begins to freeze. Where the water is calm, the water freezes into floating disks of ice. Any waves break the disks up into sugary floating crystals of frazil ice.

pack ice Floating sea ice, at least a year old, driven together to form a large single mass.

frazil Mass of newly formed, loose, needle-shaped floating ice crystals in the sea.

In summer, winds can whip at tremendous speeds across the open ice. But in winter the air near the ground will become so icy and immobile that the wind drops, and the Arctic turns eerily still.

As the winter progresses, the permanent ice sheet will spread farther and farther out from the North Pole and from the center of Greenland, eventually covering most of the Arctic Ocean. Any new pack ice that survives the following summer will turn blue as it gradually loses the salt of sea water.

The colder the weather gets, the more chunks of frazil ice freeze together to form a continuous sheet of ice called nilas. At first, nilas is clear and thinner than a glass tabletop, but as temperatures drop it turns gray in color, then white as it grows to form pack ice at least 3 ft (1 m) thick.

SHRINKING ICECAPS

Every summer a little of the Arctic ice melts only to refreeze in the fall. But over the last 25 years, global warming has warmed the air even in the Arctic. As a result, a little more ice seems to melt each summer and a little less refreezes. So the Arctic ice sheet is slowly shrinking. As ice on Greenland melts, a lot of water is added to the oceans, raising sea levels. If all Greenland's glaciers melted, every coastal city on Earth would be flooded.

AVERAGE POLAR SUMMER ICE EXTENT

The Arctic ice in summer is continuing to shrink

SEPTEMBER 1972–1990

SEPTEMBER 2005

SEPTEMBER 2030 (PROJECTED)

nilas A sheet of smooth, very thin sea ice, less than 4 in (10 cm) thick.

global warming The gradual warming of the world's climate, mostly due to pollution of the air from burning fuels such as oil.

Northern Siberia is the coldest place in the world outside Antarctica. On February 6, 1922, Verkhoyansk and Oymyakon in Siberia both recorded temperatures of -90°F (-67.8°C). Very low temperatures such as these occur when high air pressure keeps the sky clear, allowing the sun's daytime warmth to escape into the air during the long winter night.

Yet it is not the cold alone that always makes for the worst weather in this part of the world. The most severe conditions occur when bitter cold combines with strong winds and snow to create a **blizzard**. Blizzards begin with winds blowing in from the northeast, bringing icy-cold air directly from the Arctic.

By themselves, these northeast winds simply bring cold—not such a problem for those equipped to deal with it. The trouble begins when this cold air meets warm air from the south. Cold air cannot hold much moisture; warm air can. It is this combination of cold air and moisture-laden air that brings snow.

As the cold air meets the warm air, the warm air is forced upward—and as the warm air is forced up, its moisture condenses to form thick clouds. Clouds are full of ice crystals and snowflakes for most of the year this far north. But the snow typically melts to rain or sleet as it falls into warmer air.

Now, though, the snow is not falling into warmer air, but into the icy cold air that undercuts the warmer air. So it falls all the way to the ground as snow, quickly covering everything in layers of white. A blizzard, though, is very different from a snowstorm in which the snow drifts gently down.

blizzard A snowstorm lasting more than three hours with winds of 535 mph (5 kph) and visibility of less than a quarter of a mile.

SNOWFLAKES

Every snowflake has six sides and is made of up to 200 crystals, but no two are exactly alike. A snowflake's shape depends on the conditions in which it formed. Needle and rod shapes form in cold air, while warmer air creates more complicated patterns. Some snowflakes start when water drops condense on dust particles in a cold cloud. As the drop freezes, ice crystals grow on it. But when the air is very cold, snowflakes form as moisture in a cloud freezes directly to ice crystals.

Sometimes there is so much snow in the air that people cannot tell the ground from the sky. Anyone caught in a **whiteout** like this can quickly become disorientated and lose their way. If they are out in the open for long, they may freeze to death—or die from **hypothermia**, frost bite, or even suffocation.

The fierce wind not only drives the falling snow in all directions, but blasts fallen snow off the ground and hurls it through the air. Some places are stripped of their snow cover, while others are covered in deep snowdrifts that can bury livestock. Roads are quickly blocked, while the weight of snow can make buildings collapse or bring down power lines.

In a blizzard, the snow combines with blustery, piercing winds, which blow the snow along almost horizontally as it falls, hurling ice at anyone trying to walk through the storm. Visibility falls to barely 500 ft (150 m) and the wind heightens the cold of the air dramatically with a **wind chill** as low as -20°F (-6.6°C).

wind chill The colder feel of the air when it is windy; wind chill is the apparent temperature felt on exposed skin.

whiteout When windblown snow in a blizzard makes it impossible to see far or to distinguish the ground from the sky.

hypothermia When the body temperature drops below 95°F (35°C), endangering bodily functions.

CATALOG OF FROSTS

When the ground cools at night, it cools the air above it. Sometimes the air is cooled so much that moisture in it condenses to form drops of water or dew on the ground. If the night is very cold, the moisture may freeze rather than form dew, leaving a layer of sparkling ice called frost covering ground, trees, and buildings by morning. Different weather conditions bring different types of frost.

Hoar frost covers branches, leaves, and metal surfaces in icy needles

Frost is usually white because the ice crystals contain air

Hoar frost

When cool, damp air blows over icy surfaces, moisture in it can freeze instantly in spiky needles called hoar frost. Hoar frost typically occurs when air temperatures hover around 32°F (0°C) and the ground is much colder.

Ice storm

When cold rain falls on icy-cold ground, it may freeze instantly on contact and cover surfaces in a layer of clear ice. The rain is called freezing rain, and if conditions are particularly severe, and the ice covering very heavy, it is known as an ice storm.

Ice contains little air and is crystal clear if the rain freezes quickly

Frosty landscape

When a calm, clear, dry night follows a chilly winter's day, the ground may well be covered by a layer of frost by the morning. Winter nights are long, and if the air is clear any heat pumped into the ground by the cool daytime sun disperses quickly into the air. In turn, the cold ground cools the air, so that moisture in it freezes.

Conditions Air temperature below 32°F (0°C); low temperatures near the ground can create a fog.

Fact file Temperatures in Vostok, Antarctica, average -72°F (-57.8°C).

Fern frost

Frost sometimes creates wonderful patterns on cold glass. Fern frost forms on the insides of windows. First, condensation settles on the glass. Then, as the night gets colder, the condensation freezes, and as it turns to ice more crystals grow on it.

Ground frost

Ground frosts typically occur when the air cools below freezing point (32°F) (0°C). When this happens the ground is quickly covered in a layer of sugary white crystals. Ground frost may also occur when a chilly wind blows over cool ground.

Rime ice

Rime ice is a thick, shiny coating of ice. It forms when drops of water in the clouds and in fog stay liquid far below the normal freezing point because the air pressure is very low. As soon as these droplets touch a cold surface, they freeze instantly and hard.

Rime ice forms in cold clouds and fogs

Ground frost under a microscope

Frost crystal

Every frost crystal is different. Crystals form gradually, with some moisture freezing onto surfaces directly, and some freezing onto other ice crystals, making them grow in all kinds of fantastic shapes and forms.

DESERT WEATHER

The driest places in the world are deserts. Most deserts are dry either because it rains very little, or because it is so warm that evaporation is greater than rainfall. Polar regions are said to be deserts because the air is too cold to hold enough moisture for rain. Without water, they become hostile environments for life. Although some plants and animals have adapted to life in these conditions, they are scarce, and most deserts are deserted.

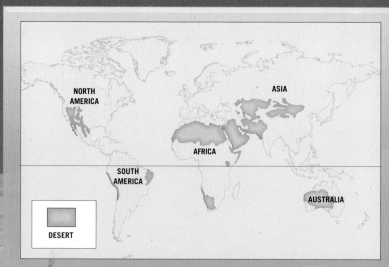

The world's largest deserts lie in the **subtropics**, between the tropics and temperate regions. The largest of all includes the Sahara and the Arabian deserts, stretching across Africa and into the Middle East. Here, the shortage of rain begins with the tropical sun that stirs up rising air currents in tropical regions.

THE WORLD'S DESERTS

Most of the world's deserts lie in the subtropics, where warm, sinking air creates very dry conditions. These include the deserts of North Africa, Australia, and the southwest United States. Cool ocean currents flowing along the western coasts of continents in the subtropics can rob air of its moisture, too, by cooling it as it flows toward the coast. West-coast deserts such as the western Sahara, Botswana's Kalahari, and the Atacama in Chile are among the driest places in the world. The Atacama is especially dry because winds from the sea dump all their moisture as rain on the peaks of the Andes, then dry out as they descend to the Atacama. There are also deserts in continental interiors, such as Asia's Gobi, which are just too far from the moisture provided by the oceans.

As they reach their upper limit, these rising air currents stream out toward the subtropics, leaving behind all their moisture (see page 13). By the time they arrive here in Arabia, they are not only dry but cooler—cool enough to sink again. As the air sinks, it begins to warm up by 22°F (10°C) for every 3,000 ft (1,000 m) it falls.

Any last trace of moisture evaporates from the sinking air as it warms. Clouds vanish and even the tiniest drop of water in the air vaporizes, leaving the sky an intense, clear, vivid blue. Clouds do sometimes appear in the sky above the desert, but they are rare. If clouds are rare, rainfall is even rarer.

With so few clouds to block it out, sunshine beats down almost unhindered. Nearly 4,000 of the 4,100 hours of daylight each year are filled with direct, strong sunlight. In fact, 90 percent of the sunshine entering the atmosphere here reaches the ground, a higher proportion than anywhere else in the world.

subtropics The region of the world that lies just outside the tropics, and which experiences tropical conditions for half the year.

Only at night is there relief from the scorching hear. Once the Sun goes down, the clear skies mean that there is no insulating blanket of cloud. The heat quickly escapes from the ground into the night air. Nights can be cool—as much as 72°F (40°C) cooler than the day. But as soon as the Sun comes up again, the temperature quickly soars.

In a few places, the wind blows away the sand to expose water-bearing rock strata. This is filled with water from wetter regions beyond the desert. Here, a small moist patch in the desert, called an oasis, may appear, and a clump of palm trees and other plants may flourish amid the dunes.

Such intense heat quickly evaporates any water in the ground—so very few plants can survive. With no water to wash away the ground and no vegetation cover, broken rock fragments pile up in many areas to create seas of sand, heaped into dunes by the winds that whip across the desert.

All this sunshine makes the Arabian Desert extremely hot. Daytime temperatures are typically more than 104°F (40°C) in the shade, and occasionally soar to 129°F (54°C). But, with few trees, there is little shade, and in direct sunshine it is even hotter—hot enough to fry an egg on a car hood.

DUST STORMS

As winds blow across the deserts, they can pick up huge quantities of sand and dust to create dust storms. In the Arabian Desert, winds from the north called shamals blow for a month or so twice each year. The shamals pick up millions of tons of sand to create blinding dust storms. Sometimes, these storms cover vast areas in dense clouds of swirling dust. At other times, they create localized whirlwinds called dust devils, or *jinn* (above).

Most extreme weather, such as hurricanes and monsoons, is associated with too much rain. But every now and then some parts of the world suffer from too little rain. In temperate regions, 15 days without any rain is classified as a drought. Places in Southern Africa, however, may go many months without rain.

Rains sometimes fail when too little water vapor rises into the colder regions of the air to condense into clouds. This happens when the air pressure is high and air falls instead of rising. When a high-pressure system stays over a region for some time, it can block out rain-bringing weather and cause drought.

Sometimes, **high-pressure systems** are locked in place by jet streams—powerful winds in the upper atmosphere. Occasionally, shifts in ocean currents far away can have the same effect by disrupting global atmospheric circulation. The **El Niño** current in the Pacific Ocean may affect Africa in this way.

Drought does not come suddenly, and there is no one moment when a drought starts. Instead, its effects creep in gradually as each day passes without rain. If the weather is cool, many rainless months can pass with little noticeable effect because water evaporates slowly from the ground and **transpiration** from plants is small.

Unfortunately, summer days in Southern Africa are scorching, with temperatures often more than 104°F (40°C). The heat quickly draws any water from soil and plants. Grass turns straw-colored as it lets its leaves die to save water for its roots. Trees with deep roots and waxy leaves designed to cut water loss stay green longer.

high-pressure systems Large and persistent areas of high atmospheric pressure in which air is sinking and winds are flowing outward.

El Niño A reversal of ocean currents off the western coast of South America leading to a disruption of global wind circulation.

transpiration The evaporation of water from plants through pores in their leaves and stems.

Sometimes the drought goes on so long that the plants and soil may never recover. All that is left is a bare plain of dust. The region becomes a desert—a process called desertification. With luck, though, the weather will change, the rains will return, the plants will grow again, and the region will gradually return to life.

For a while, water can still be found in waterholes supplied by underground springs, or in rivers flowing from wetter regions. But, as the drought goes on, springs no longer replenished by rain dry up, and the waterholes turn to mud. Even the rivers may vanish to leave empty stream beds.

Winds, now unhindered by vegetation, whip across the ground, speeding up the drying of the soil. Before long, they strip away the dusty topsoil to leave even the deep soil naked to the searing sun. As soil dries out, it shrinks. Soon, cracks appear in the ground as patches contract to form a crazy-paving effect.

Gradually, though, more and more plants die from lack of water. As they die, more of the soil is left exposed to the baking sun—and any moisture it contains then evaporates away that much quicker. So as the drought progresses, the dry topsoil, normally held together by moisture and vegetation, turns to dust.

DEADLY DROUGHT

Drought caused by lack of rain is known as a "meteorological drought." A "hydrological drought" occurs when rivers and wells run dry or are overused. An "agricultural drought" is when soil dries out too much for crops to grow, perhaps through overintense farming. Whatever the causes, the effect can be devastating. Grazing animals, which rely on water for drinking and grass for food, die by the thousand. Crops fail, the ground turns to dust, and famine becomes a reality.

STORIES OF DROUGHT

DARFUR, SUDAN

Even in areas where there is enough water to keep animals alive, the military conflict often prevents farmers from reaching their herds, so cattle die by the thousand.

In the once-moist south, the soil is often parched and baked solid, making it almost impossible for farmers to have a decent harvest.

For the last 20 years, few places in the world have suffered more from drought than the southern fringes of the Sahara Desert in Africa. Most especially hit is the region called Darfur in southwestern Sudan. Darfur is prone to drought because it is always dry for at least half the year. The area relies on the annual rains to fill the water holes and streams and make the grass grow. Toward its northern edge, it gets drier and drier, and vegetation gets sparser and sparser until it merges into the Sahara Desert. If the rains fail, the edge of the desert spreads farther and farther south.

Riddle of the drought

Experts argue over what has brought drought to this region so often. Some link it to changes in ocean currents. Others believe an effect of the Sun or El Niño is to blame (see page 52). Some put it down to shifts in the jet streams that alter the seasonal movement of the ITCZ (see page 13)—an annual phenomenon that should normally bring the rain. A few think global warming may be at the heart of it. Yet there is no doubt that human activities have played their part, too.

Fragile farmland

As farming has become more commercial, so more marginal land has been brought into cultivation, putting pressure on water resources. As more land has been brought into cultivation, so livestock that used to roam widely has been confined to smaller areas. In the past, herders would graze their cattle a while then move on, leaving the grass time to recover. Now grass is frequently overgrazed. If the grass is not allowed to recover, it dies, along with other vegetation. This is not only bad in itself but also reduces rainfall by robbing the air of the moisture provided by plants, so making the problem worse.

> "These are the people who have died since the last rain. When the rain comes again, this is all washed away."
>
> *Darfurian villager standing next to rows of makeshift graves dug in sand*

Two tribes

It was a situation like this that started the nightmare of droughts in Darfur. In the moister south, the farmers are mostly African in origin. They are settled in villages and grow crops. In the drier north, the farmers are mostly Arab nomadic herdsmen, and only move their cattle south in the dry season. In the past, both nomads and crop farmers got along well. Then, in the early 1980s, the region was hit by the first of a series of droughts. Before long, millions of people were facing famine, and huge amounts of international aid did little to relieve the suffering. But worse was to come, as the herdsmen and crop farmers began to compete for the steadily shrinking areas of moist land.

To escape conflict *and famine, hundreds of thousands of people trekked long distances on foot through heat and dust—only to find the relief camps had none of the aid they hoped for.*

International aid *agencies brought vital food and medical supplies in the early stages of the famine, but the war made it increasingly hard for them to do their work.*

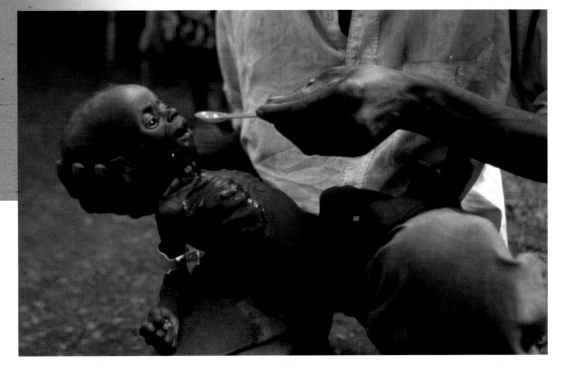

Biased government

At first, disputes were settled satisfactorily by village elders. But the government then decided it was best if it handled disputes. Unfortunately, it soon became clear to the African crop farmers that they would always lose out because the government was Arab-dominated. As the droughts got worse, so the conflicts grew more intense.

War

In 2003, a group of African farmers rebelled against the government. Arab soldiers called the Janjaweed ("devils on horseback") moved in to suppress the rebellion. The conflict spiraled out of control and the problems brought by famine were compounded by the problems of war. Suddenly it

became too dangerous for the aid agencies to reach many places, and people were robbed even of this help. A small peacekeeping force made of troops from African nations could do little, so the United Nations asked if it could step in and keep the peace. The Sudanese government refused, and so the conflict and the effects of drought continued. Hundreds of thousands fled to neighboring Chad, while millions more faced famine and worse in Darfur. Today, there is still no adequate aid reaching Darfur.

> ## "Even if we could go back, what is left there now?"
>
> *Darfurian farmer in a refugee camp*

Children suffering *from lack of food are not only undernourished but prone to all kinds of diseases. A shortage of medicines makes the situation even worse.*

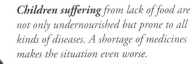

Members of the Janjaweed militia, *seen here, have been accused of many crimes in Darfur, including murder.*

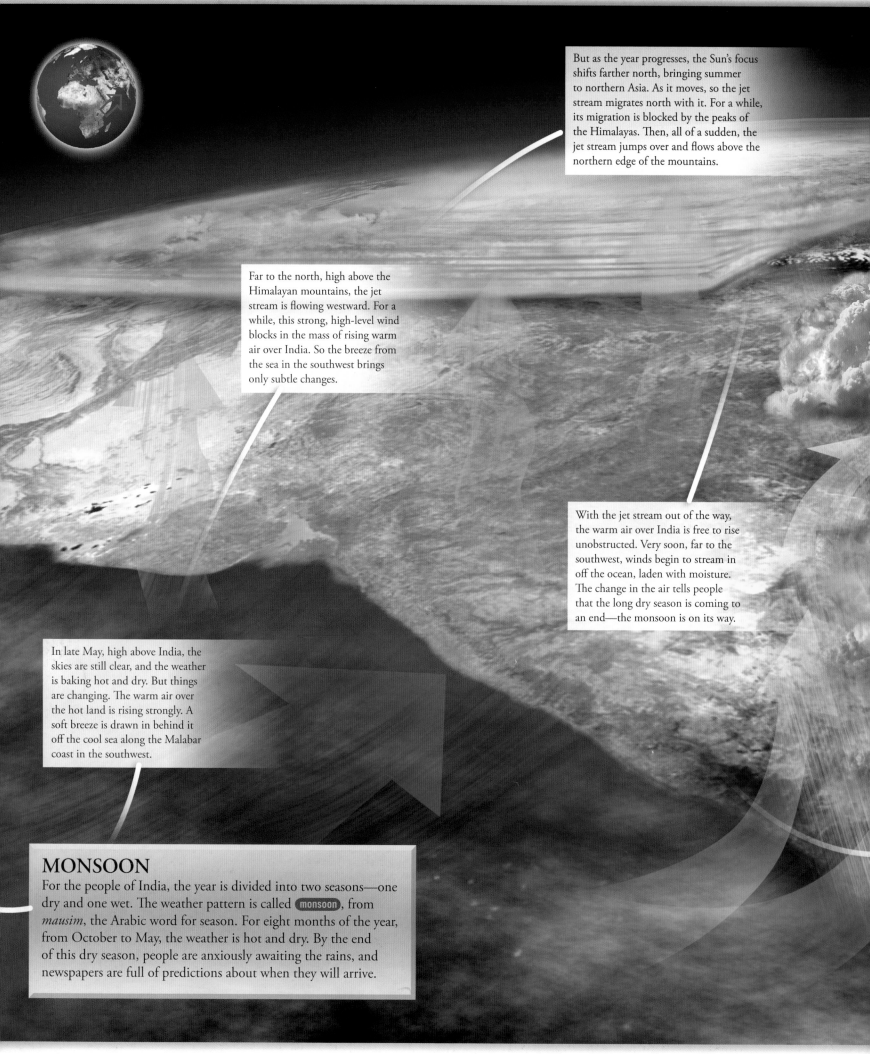

But as the year progresses, the Sun's focus shifts farther north, bringing summer to northern Asia. As it moves, so the jet stream migrates north with it. For a while, its migration is blocked by the peaks of the Himalayas. Then, all of a sudden, the jet stream jumps over and flows above the northern edge of the mountains.

Far to the north, high above the Himalayan mountains, the jet stream is flowing westward. For a while, this strong, high-level wind blocks in the mass of rising warm air over India. So the breeze from the sea in the southwest brings only subtle changes.

With the jet stream out of the way, the warm air over India is free to rise unobstructed. Very soon, far to the southwest, winds begin to stream in off the ocean, laden with moisture. The change in the air tells people that the long dry season is coming to an end—the monsoon is on its way.

In late May, high above India, the skies are still clear, and the weather is baking hot and dry. But things are changing. The warm air over the hot land is rising strongly. A soft breeze is drawn in behind it off the cool sea along the Malabar coast in the southwest.

MONSOON

For the people of India, the year is divided into two seasons—one dry and one wet. The weather pattern is called monsoon, from *mausim*, the Arabic word for season. For eight months of the year, from October to May, the weather is hot and dry. By the end of this dry season, people are anxiously awaiting the rains, and newspapers are full of predictions about when they will arrive.

monsoon A seasonal shift in the prevailing wind direction that brings changes in the weather to the countries of southern Asia.

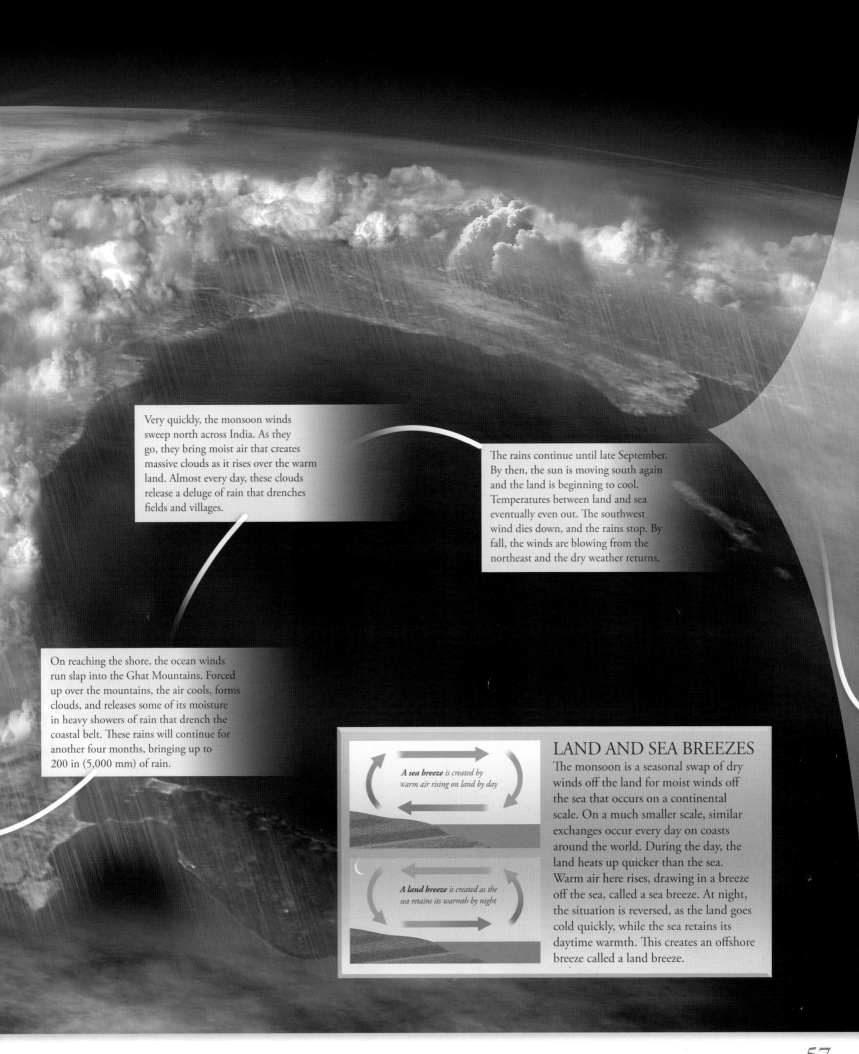

Very quickly, the monsoon winds sweep north across India. As they go, they bring moist air that creates massive clouds as it rises over the warm land. Almost every day, these clouds release a deluge of rain that drenches fields and villages.

The rains continue until late September. By then, the sun is moving south again and the land is beginning to cool. Temperatures between land and sea eventually even out. The southwest wind dies down, and the rains stop. By fall, the winds are blowing from the northeast and the dry weather returns.

On reaching the shore, the ocean winds run slap into the Ghat Mountains. Forced up over the mountains, the air cools, forms clouds, and releases some of its moisture in heavy showers of rain that drench the coastal belt. These rains will continue for another four months, bringing up to 200 in (5,000 mm) of rain.

LAND AND SEA BREEZES

A sea breeze is created by warm air rising on land by day

A land breeze is created as the sea retains its warmth by night

The monsoon is a seasonal swap of dry winds off the land for moist winds off the sea that occurs on a continental scale. On a much smaller scale, similar exchanges occur every day on coasts around the world. During the day, the land heats up quicker than the sea. Warm air here rises, drawing in a breeze off the sea, called a sea breeze. At night, the situation is reversed, as the land goes cold quickly, while the sea retains its daytime warmth. This creates an offshore breeze called a land breeze.

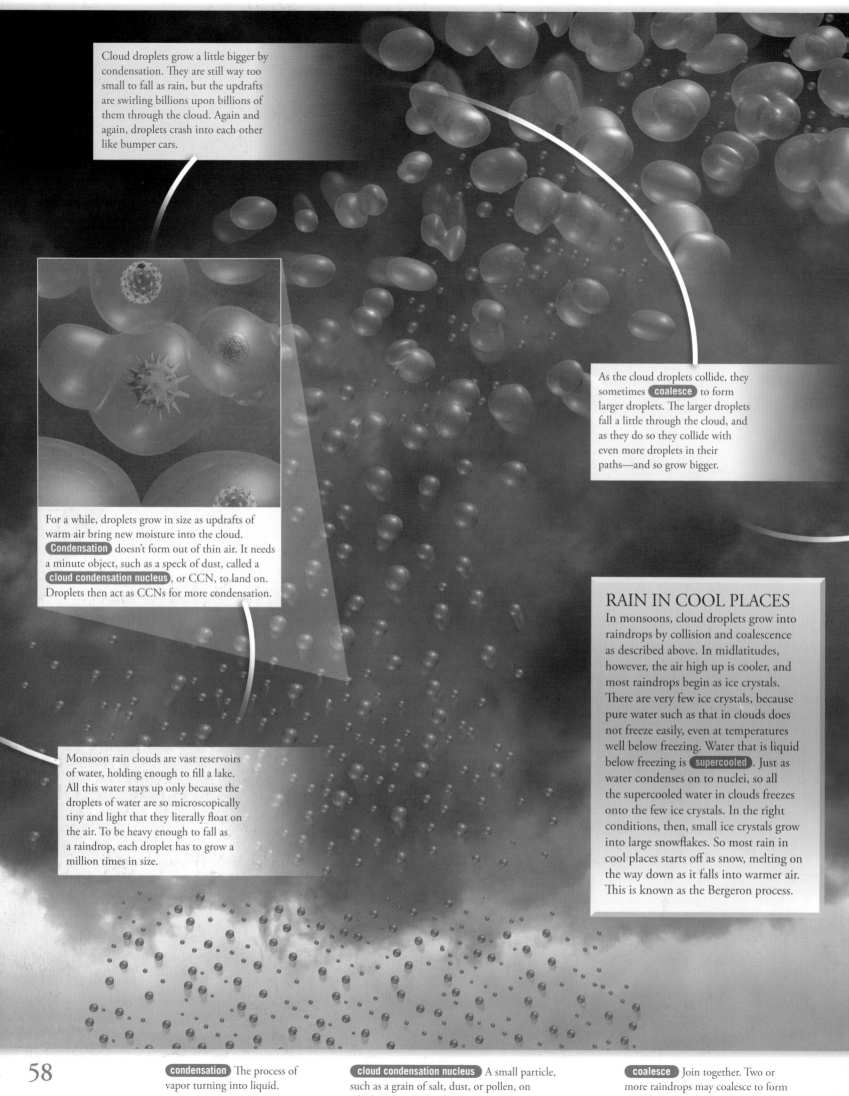

Cloud droplets grow a little bigger by condensation. They are still way too small to fall as rain, but the updrafts are swirling billions upon billions of them through the cloud. Again and again, droplets crash into each other like bumper cars.

For a while, droplets grow in size as updrafts of warm air bring new moisture into the cloud. **Condensation** doesn't form out of thin air. It needs a minute object, such as a speck of dust, called a **cloud condensation nucleus**, or CCN, to land on. Droplets then act as CCNs for more condensation.

As the cloud droplets collide, they sometimes **coalesce** to form larger droplets. The larger droplets fall a little through the cloud, and as they do so they collide with even more droplets in their paths—and so grow bigger.

Monsoon rain clouds are vast reservoirs of water, holding enough to fill a lake. All this water stays up only because the droplets of water are so microscopically tiny and light that they literally float on the air. To be heavy enough to fall as a raindrop, each droplet has to grow a million times in size.

RAIN IN COOL PLACES

In monsoons, cloud droplets grow into raindrops by collision and coalescence as described above. In midlatitudes, however, the air high up is cooler, and most raindrops begin as ice crystals. There are very few ice crystals, because pure water such as that in clouds does not freeze easily, even at temperatures well below freezing. Water that is liquid below freezing is **supercooled**. Just as water condenses on to nuclei, so all the supercooled water in clouds freezes onto the few ice crystals. In the right conditions, then, small ice crystals grow into large snowflakes. So most rain in cool places starts off as snow, melting on the way down as it falls into warmer air. This is known as the Bergeron process.

condensation The process of vapor turning into liquid.

cloud condensation nucleus A small particle, such as a grain of salt, dust, or pollen, on which water can condense inside a cloud.

coalesce Join together. Two or more raindrops may coalesce to form a single drop.

Soon, many falling raindrops are large—a fraction of an inch, or about a millimeter, across. They are not teardrop-shaped but round, and if they grow any larger, they become shaped like hamburgers. The largest raindrops are about 0.2 in (5 mm) across and shaped like parachutes.

Eventually, the droplets grow into raindrops and the updrafts that hold them die down. Raindrops begin to fall through the cloud, hitting other drops on the way down and growing bigger. As they fall, they clear a path through the cloud and gather more drops in their wake.

All these falling raindrops cool the air and create a downdraft. This not only speeds them on their way down, but also brings ever more drops in. They plummet through the bottom of the cloud like water bursting from a soggy paper bag, and fall as a sudden torrent of rain.

supercooled When water stays liquid well below its freezing point—32°F (0°C).

As the monsoon rains continue, they fill the vast network of rivers that flow across the lowlands of Bangladesh. On the wettest days in September, up to 16 in (400 mm) of rain a day falls on the hills and mountains to the north that feed these rivers.

Much of this water is channeled into three great rivers, the Ganges, Brahmaputra, and Meghna. When these mighty rivers join up for the final 44 mile- (70 km-) journey to the sea, they carry 1.3 billion gal (5,000,000 cu m) of water a second, more than any other river in the world, including the Amazon.

As the weeks go by, the level of water in the rivers steadily rises, and they are soon nearing the top of the levées built to confine them. It is touch and go whether the levées can hold all the water in. People in the surrounding lands begin to watch anxiously.

Then, particularly heavy rain in the hills fills the rivers to bursting. Just as the water reaches the lowlands, torrential rain comes down here, too. Suddenly, there are huge amounts of water with nowhere to flow. Water spills from the rivers and floods vast areas of land.

levées Natural or artificial embankments that contain a river.

MIXED BLESSING
Stranded Bangladeshis are seen here watching their flooded fields from the rooftops. In situations as bad as this, food aid is flown in. Ironically, the monsoon rains that bring such misery are also vital for the country's food supply. The planting of basic crops such as rice, corn, and soybeans only begins when the first monsoon rains fall in June each year.

Eventually, though, the rains peter out and the water drains away from the land. As the floods slowly subside, a chaos of mud, garbage, debris, and broken houses is revealed. Gradually, the mess is cleared—ready for another year.

Conditions quickly worsen. Entire villages may be cut off from food and medical supplies for weeks on end. Ironically, there is not even water to drink. The stagnant flood water, already poisoned by chemicals washed off the land and from industry, is quickly infected with diseases.

Fields are quickly swamped, houses are cut off or even washed away, power lines are broken, roads are destroyed, and vast areas are inundated by the rising waters. Hundreds of people, thousands of farm animals, and countless wild creatures drown. Survivors are left clinging desperately to trees and house roofs.

CATALOG OF CLIMATE TYPES

Everywhere has its own typical weather, or climate. The nearer we are to the equator, the warmer it is. At the equator, the Sun climbs high in the sky, giving warm, tropical climates. Farther away, the Sun is lower in the sky, giving more moderate, or temperate, climates. At the poles, the Sun stays so low in the sky that the climate is always cold. Within these three broad bands, climates vary in how seasonal they are, and in wetness.

Rainforest
The tropics are warm, with temperatures often averaging more than 80°F (27°C) all year round. Where it is wet, it tends to be very wet, since the warm air takes up huge amounts of moisture. Steamy tropical rainforests flourish in this hot, moist climate.

THE SEASONS

Spring
As the Earth travels around the Sun, sunlight strikes it at different angles. In temperate regions, this creates four seasons. In spring, days and nights are equally long, the Sun climbs only moderately high. Days are warm, but nights are cool and the weather showery.

Summer
In summer, the Sun climbs to its maximum height in the sky, so its rays are strong. Days last much longer than nights, too. So the weather is warm or even hot. It rains much less often, but when it does it typically comes in sudden thunderstorms late in the day.

Fall
By the fall, the Sun is sinking in the sky again. Days and nights are again equally long. Days are still warm, but the air is less dry. Nights can be cold, and moisture in the air may condense to form mists. The weather is often stormy and wet.

Winter
By midwinter, the Sun is very low in the sky even at midday. The nights are very long, too. Days are so short that the air never gets the chance to heat up fully. So the weather is frequently cold. Night frosts are common, and it may snow.

Mediterranean
Coastal regions between the tropics and the temperate zone often have "Mediterranean" climates, because they are typical of the lands around the Mediterranean Sea. Summers are hot and dry. Most rain falls in winter, when it is cool, but it is never really cold.

Savanna
Many places in the tropics lie along the ITCZ, the line where winds from the north and south meet. As this line shifts through the year, it brings rain or drought. The dry season is too dry for trees to flourish, so these regions tend to have wide grasslands called savanna.

Steppe
Oceans store heat and moderate the difference between summer and winter. Far from the sea, the interiors of continents swing between hot summers and bitter winters. They may be dry— too dry for forests—and take the form of grasslands called steppes and prairies.

Climate zones map

The warmth of a region's climate depends on how close it is to the equator. But oceans and mountain ranges have a huge influence on climate, too, so the pattern is complicated, with many local variations, as this map shows. Coastal areas tend to be damper and cooler, for instance, while continental interiors far inland tend to be drier and more extreme, with hot summers and cold winters.

POLAR
TUNDRA
SUBARCTIC
CONTINENTAL
TEMPERATE
SUBTROPICAL
MEDITERRANEAN
SEMI ARID
ARID
TROPICAL
EQUATORIAL
MOUNTAIN

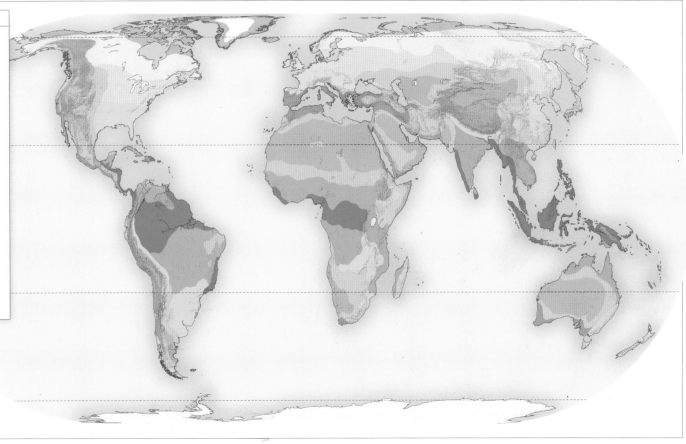

Tundra

In the cold regions north of Siberia, Scandinavia, Canada, and Alaska, winter temperatures drop below -14°F (-10°C). Conifers are the only trees that grow here. In the far north, not even these grow, creating landscapes of moss and grass called tundra.

Temperate

Much of the US, northern Europe, and Japan has a climate that is rarely extreme, which is why it is called temperate. But there are four distinct seasons. Trees are typically deciduous in temperate regions, losing their leaves for the cold, dry days of winter.

Mountain climates

Everywhere in the world, the air gets cooler and the weather tougher with altitude. Mountain tops are stormy and cold. Above a certain height, called the snow line, peaks are permanently covered in snow. The nearer you go to the poles, the lower the snow line is.

INDEX

A page number in **bold** refers to the main entry for that subject

ACKNOWLEDGMENTS

Dorling Kindersley would like to thank Chris Bernstein for the index; Margaret Parrish for text Americanization.

Picture Credits
The publisher would like to thank the following for their kind permission to reproduce their photographs:

(Abbreviations key: t=top, b=below, r=right, l=left, c=center, a=above)

Alamy Images: blickwinkel 50-51
Corbis: Lynsey Addario 54tr; Bettmann 30cr; 31t; Nic Bothma/epa 55br; Dallas Morning News/Rick Gershon 23br; Jon Davies 43bl; Khaled el fiqi/epa 55tr; Lowell Georgia 49tl; Eric Gilbert 48l; Jim Reed Photography/Eric Nguyen 30l; Ron Sanford 43t; Shepard Sherbell 11br; Hans Strand 44-45; Liba Taylor 54bl
DK Images: Stephen Oliver 10tr
Empics Ltd: AP 31cr; AP/David J. Phillip 20-21; AP/John Russell 28-29
FLPA: Peter Davey 53br; Jim Reed 39t
Getty Images: Aurora/Peter Essick 60-61; Christian Aid/Mike Goldwater 52-53; The Image Bank/Stephen Frink 24t; National Geographic/Joel Sartore 51br; Science Faction/NASA JSC 16-17
Masterfile: Hans Blohm 38-39; Allan Davey 41cr; John Foster 33b
NASA: 1, 2-3, 4t, 4c, 4b, 5tl, 5tc, 5tr, 5cr, 5b, 7cr, 11tr, 11tc, 11bl, 22tl, 64-65, 66-67, 68; Landsat 22tr, 22cr
naturepl.com: Asgeir Helgestad 46-47
NOAA: 31cl, 31b
Panos Pictures: Dieter Telemans 61t
Victor Pasko/Penn State University 41t
Photolibrary: Warren Faidley 40-41; Ifa-Bilderteam GmbH 62tl, 62ca, 62cb, 64bl
Reuters: David J. Phillip 23b; Shannon Stapleton 23tr
Science Photo Library: Martin Dohrn 54tl; Bernard Edmaier 49br; Jim Reed Photography/Mike Umscheid 48tr; Larry West 48cr
Still Pictures: Alpha Presse/Larry MacDougal 32-33
TopFoto.co.uk: Chalasani/UN 55cr
Courtesy of US Navy: Airman Jeremy L. Grisham 22b

Jacket images: Front and Back:
Science Photo Library: Ted Kinsman (b/g). Front: Science Photo Library: Gordon Garradd cr

All other images © Dorling Kindersley
For further information see: www.dkimages.com

LONDON, NEW YORK, MELBOURNE,
MUNICH, AND DELHI

Consultant Lisa Burke

For Tall Tree Ltd
Editor David John
Designers Ed Simkins, Ralph Pitchford, Jonathan Vipond

For DK
Senior Editor Claire Nottage
Senior Art Editor Jim Green
Managing Editor Linda Esposito
Managing Art Editor Diane Thistlethwaite
Jacket Manager Sophia M. Tampakopoulos Turner

DTP Coordinator Siu Yin Chan

Publishing Manager Andrew Macintyre
Category Publisher Laura Buller

Picture Research Fran Vargo, Rose Horridge
Production Erica Rosen
Jacket Design Neal Cobourne
Jacket Editor Mariza O'Keeffe

Illustrators Candylab, Andrew Kerr

First American edition, 2007
Published in the United States by
DK Publishing, Inc. 375 Hudson Street
New York, New York 10014

06 07 08 09 10 10 9 8 7 6 5 4 3 2 1

A Cataloging-in-Publication record for this book
is available from the Library of Congress.

ISBN 978-0-75662-837-6

Colour reproduction by Colourscan, Singapore
Printed and bound in China by Hung Hing
Discover more at
www.dk.com

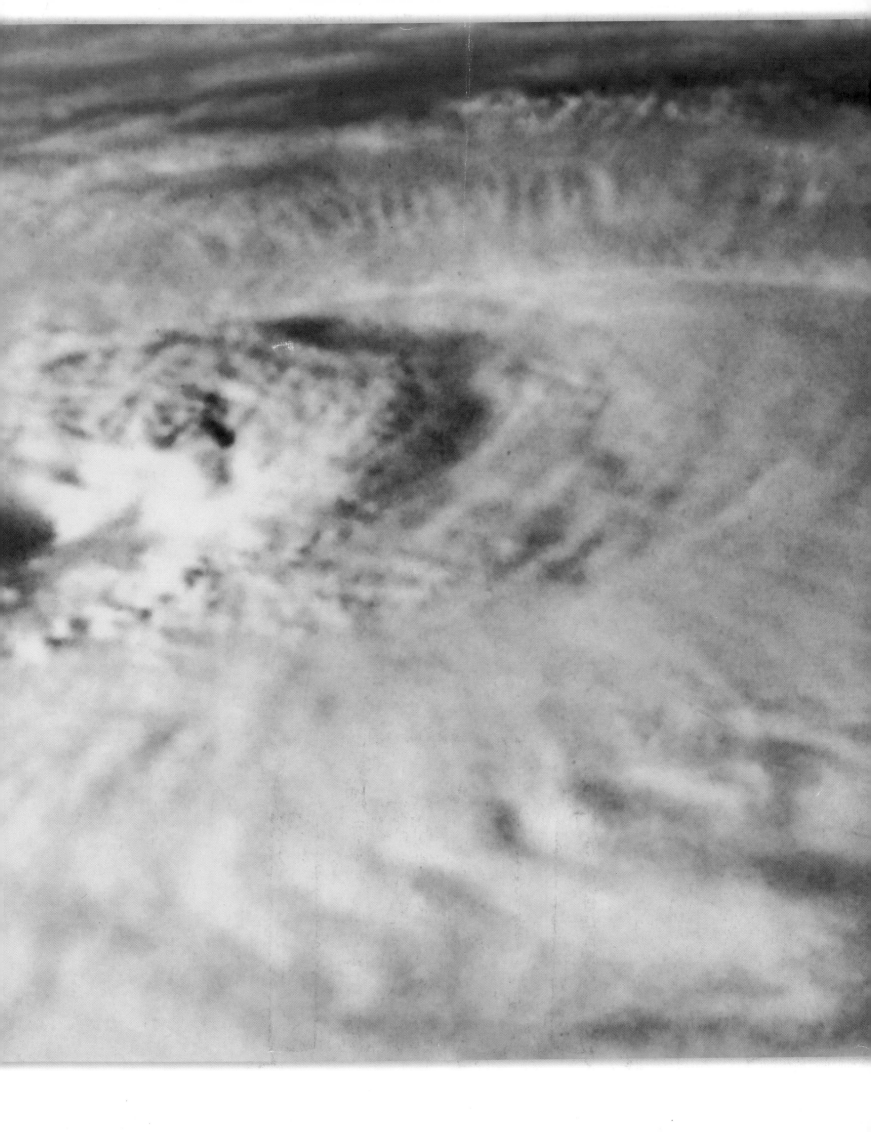